modern
freezer meals

modern freezer meals

Simple Recipes to Cook Now and Freeze for Later

Ali Rosen | James Beard- and Emmy-nominated
founder and host of *Potluck with Ali*

Skyhorse Publishing

This book is dedicated to my parents, Susan and Robert Rosen, for instilling in me the values of working hard, being kind, giving back, and loving your family to the fullest. Everything I accomplish is because of the example you both set.

contents

how to freeze

Do This If You Do Nothing Else

Here's the cheat sheet for anyone who doesn't want to take the time to read the following chapter. Please, please just do these things if you do nothing else:

- Let your food fully cool down before freezing it.
- Freeze in single servings, not in giant blocks.
- Make sure no air is touching your food and it is sealed as tightly as possible.

Read on to learn more—but just these simple rules will make your frozen food worlds better.

start with a new mindset

We are, thankfully, living in an era of freshness. We've discarded the cloak of canned foods and oversalted TV dinners and now we relish in our ability to find the most local and unique products to turn into our evening meals and weekend projects. But here's the problem: there's still just not enough time in the day.

It's the modern cooking rub. We want to cook better and eat better than our parents did, but we don't actually have the consistent time to devote to it. The number of nights that I've looked around in my fridge to make a salad out of sad leftover ingredients are too innumerable to count. And yet we've all gotten into the mindset that if it comes out of the freezer then it must be the worst kind of leftover. It's a necessary failure. But why can't both things be true—why can't we love our fresh, seasonal foods and also sometimes need to pull something out of the freezer?

I wasn't always a freezer convert. In fact, I was the kind of person who was surprised when anyone used them for something other than ice cream and gin. Who didn't have time to throw a piece of fish in the oven for twelve minutes with a bit of lemon and some fresh herbs? But then life happened. I had a kid and suddenly the time it took to actually get to the grocery store to buy the fish was sometimes more than what I had capacity for. My mom went through chemo, and suddenly freezing food was the only way to be there for her on the days I couldn't physically be. The freezer started looking like the nice boy from high school who asked you out but (at the time), wasn't exciting enough to say yes to. The freezer wasn't sexy or cool, but it was there when I wanted to visit friends with new babies and give them meals to parcel out over the coming weeks. I no longer minded taking a meal out of the freezer when I was working late and barely had five minutes to heat something up.

My life as a person obsessed with peak summer tomatoes didn't have to impinge on my growing love for the freezer. It could enhance it. I started to make more and more food with the freezer in mind. At first it started out with the typical freezer fare—a lasagna here, a soup there—but soon I started to branch out. I was putting skewered shrimp and soy sauce glazed snap peas in the freezer just to see how they would eventually thaw. I was testing whether crab cakes actually cooked *better* from frozen (they do, by the way). I was making so many batches of cookies in various forms that I became a pretty popular neighbor to have around.

To my surprise and delight, a lot more food could handle the freezer than what I'd been conditioned to believe. And it was so much easier than my image of hours of batch cooking. Most of the time it just meant making a few extra portions of what I was already doing. It barely added any time and in return I always had something on hand to eat. My days of ordering in just because I was tired were over. Every time I wanted to eat something a quick trip to the freezer held delights I'd forgotten about from days or weeks earlier. And it actually *saved* seasonality for later: the flavors of summer corn and berries could all be kept frozen in time until some cold winter day needed a bit of brightness to be summoned.

We have reembraced so many of our grandparents' traditions—canning, pickling, fermenting—so what is the holdup on the freezer?

Because of this dated mindset, truly the most important place to begin when thinking about freezer food is to eliminate your previous notions about what can and cannot be frozen. There are certainly indulgences here, but the freezer doesn't have to mean unhealthy and it certainly doesn't have to mean you can't pair it with something fresh. The easiest dinner for me is to pull something flavorful out of the freezer and pair it with a quick salad of veggies and greens from the fridge.

So, get comfortable with it. There is a range when it comes to freezer food. Some things work better (baked goods like scones and cheese puffs, anyone?) and some feel the same (hello, braised meats). Others, like pastas and rice, are never *quite* as good, but if stored properly they can really surprise you. Some things will never translate and that's okay. This is about making your life easier, not eating every single thing out of your freezer.

The other thing I want to emphasize is that better ingredients still make better food. There is a reason why some of the best summer fruit is made into jam and why frozen vegetables often have the highest vitamin content—using the freezer is just a more modern way of preserving our food, like generations have done before us. And having tomato soup in November is a bonus. The goal here often is to eat a meal and save a meal—you *should* be eating these items at peak times and without the freezer. But saving the leftovers for later is also the name of the game.

To make sifting through this book a little easier we've got a few badges to guide you:

Look for these when you want something quicker and easier. You'll be shocked that most of these recipes fall into at least one category.

But beyond the badges, there are still a few rules and tricks to make your life easier. The rest of this chapter is all about how to approach freezing. The best recipes can come undone if you don't have the basic techniques to use your freezer to the best of its ability. Make your dinners easier by opening your freezer door.

cool it

There is nothing more you can do for the quality of your frozen food than allowing it to cool down before freezing it. Make sure anything is fully room temperature (or even cold) before it goes near the freezer. Stick it in the fridge overnight if you don't have time to wait, but whatever you do, do *not* freeze hot food. Let me say it again because it bears constant repeating: Do not freeze anything that is warmer than room temperature. This might sound a bit hyperbolic, but if you understand just the basics of the science of freezing, you'll never make this mistake again.

When food is freezing, ice crystals form and lock in the food's cellular structure to preserve it. It might seem like all ice is the same, but ice crystals can form in different sizes. The smaller the crystals, the less damage to the food because less of its cellular structure is changing. The larger the crystals, the more damage can be to the cell membranes—and that damage is what causes changes in texture that you can taste once you defrost. The faster a food freezes, the smaller and more uniform the crystals.

Every type of food is made up of a mixture of different substances with different freezing points, or the temperature at which a substance fully freezes. We all know that water freezes at 32°F. But think of that bottle of vodka you have in your freezer that never actually freezes—that's because alcohol has a much lower freezing point, so a conventional freezer would never turn it into a solid block. With food, you are dealing with a multitude of substances within each item or dish that freeze at slightly different points. For example, most fish are 70 to 80 percent water, then mostly fat and protein. Since fat and protein freeze at a much lower temperature, the water is freezing first and has time to expand.[1] And that expansion creates those larger crystals that damage our food.

So, cool it down. Portion it out so that it cools faster. Let it sit on the counter for as long as you can before moving it into the fridge (try not to put super-hot food in the fridge either because that could warm up the food around it). Once it is fully cool or even cold, that's when you can start the freezing process. Give food space in the freezer and try to use a shelf that isn't too crowded so that everything freezes as quickly as possible. The colder it starts, the faster it will freeze and the better your food will taste. The science certainly isn't simple. But the concept is: cool it.

---

1   Murray, J. and Burt, J.R. 2001. The Composition of Fish. Torry Advisory Note No. 38, Ministry of Technology. Torry Research Station, U.K.
    Dawson, Paul, Al-Jeddawi, Wesam and Remington, Nanne. 2018. Effect of Freezing on the Shelf Life of Salmon. *International Journal of Food Science.*

portions, portions, portions

Now that we've established that getting food to freeze as quickly as possible is the best way to keep it as fresh as possible, the next aspect that will impact the quality of food is the actual size. A giant block of food takes longer to freeze. Portion that giant block into eight smaller blocks and suddenly everything moves much faster.

But it's not just the quality on the freezing side that we are looking out for—it's also the amount of heat we need to get it hot again. Some items you can allow to defrost, but most of the time we just want to stick whatever we are eating right from the freezer into the microwave or oven. And the larger the item is, the longer it takes to heat, eroding freshness once again. Especially for items like pastas and meats—which need a bit more care in the freezer—the less additional cooking you have to do on the back end, the better they will taste.

Beyond that, portions just generally make your life easier by giving you more choice. If you want to make a quick lunch and you've stored your soup in a giant eight-serving block, then you're going to have to eat all of that soup within a few days of unfreezing it. If you stored it in a container that is the perfect individual meal size, all you have to do is grab that one portion and throw it straight into the microwave for a few minutes. Whatever small amount of time you spend dividing your meals on the front end will be handsomely rewarded in the ease of getting a single portion of food onto the table.

For items that can't easily be thrown into containers without sticking together, like cookie dough balls or pigs in a blanket, you want to spread them out on a sheet pan with parchment paper and freeze them for a few hours first. Once they are completely frozen, then you can put them all into a container and easily grab one piece later without worrying about everything sticking together. You'll thank yourself later when you can heat up one cookie for an afternoon snack without having to make the entire batch (but no judgement if you want to eat the entire batch just because!). By portioning your food, you give yourself more options—and isn't that what the freezer is all about?

air is not your friend

Once your food is frozen, there is only one remaining enemy: air.

Freezer burn is not inevitable. If you've pulled something out of the back of your freezer only to find that it looks like a gray mess of icicles, then your issue is probably more to do with storage than time. The dreaded freezer burn is a result of food losing moisture because oxygen has moved in to replace it, leaving behind a dish that has less flavor and is a lot drier and tougher than intended. But if you can keep a tight seal around your food, you block moisture from leaving and air from entering. So, wrap it up as tight and in as many layers as you can.

As to what you should wrap your food in, I'm going to share something perhaps a bit controversial: the actual container you use doesn't actually make that big of a difference as long as it isn't porous. Freezer bags, silicone bags, tempered glass containers,

heavy-duty foil, and heavy-duty plastic wrap all hold up with pretty much the same consistency. They each have their benefits: bags and wraps can adapt to any size; a tempered glass or other stable container can often mean going straight from the freezer to the microwave or oven. But in general, the amount of air left over is really the culprit of any frozen food's demise. You can use the heaviest duty bag, but if you don't press all the air out of it, then the container itself doesn't matter. Make sure to eliminate air and use materials that are made for the freezer and you're on your way to frozen food perfection.

A few things to keep in mind depending on the type of containers you use:

Tempered Glass and Other Containers
If you are using a static container, just remember that liquid expands when frozen. You don't want to leave a lot of air, but you do want to leave about ½" of headroom, especially for items like soup, otherwise your lids or containers could break. You can cover the surface with plastic wrap, then place the lid on top if you are particularly worried about freezer burn.

I love these for the convenience of taking them straight from the freezer to the microwave or oven, but just be sure that whatever glass-like or plastic-like container you are using is actually made for these purposes. Freezer-safe, oven-safe, and microwave-safe are all different standards and you should ideally be getting containers that can do all three so that you're not changing containers every time you heat things up.

Resealable Plastic Bags, Plastic Wrap, and Aluminum Foil

Heavy duty matters with this category, because thinner bags and wraps often are more porous than you might think. Check that whatever you're storing in is heavy duty (and if it says it is freezer-safe that's even better), but don't get hung up on a particular material. The heaviness and freezer-readiness are what matter most.

Another issue that people often have, especially with plastic bags, is that they are not seen as sustainable. The easiest way to replicate these items is to buy the reusable versions—silicone reusable bags or beeswax wrappers are great (but the wrappers are a bit porous, so just make sure to double up). But my favorite trick? Just reuse your regular plastic bags and wrap. You should really think of them as reusable anyway. You can rinse out a plastic bag and use it in the freezer time and again. If you can get into that mindset you don't need to worry about purchasing new containers.

Vacuum Sealers

The best containers that have come out in recent years are the ones that easily use vacuum sealing to remove any additional air from a container. Particularly if you are storing for longer-term and doing a ton of freezer meals, these can be worth it, especially as costs have gone down so dramatically in recent years. It's not an essential by any means (and especially if you are using items within a month or two, you may not see much of a difference), but this is definitely one product that does what it says.

but labels definitely *are* your friend

It is so much easier to take thirty extra seconds to write on a label than it is to stare at the bottom of a frosted-over container trying to remember what exactly you cooked two months ago. Labels do not have to be fancy or complicated—I usually just use a piece of tape and a Sharpie. I write down one or two words to jog my memory, then, most importantly, the month and year. That little action should be the bare minimum if you are using your freezer on a frequent basis. But there are a few other simple additions that can dramatically improve the ease of your day with just a little forward planning.

The first is that anything needing a specific time and temperature to reheat should have that written on the label. A dish that gets thrown in the microwave and stirred every minute or so doesn't need extra time reminders, but a pork chop certainly does. Not having to pull up the recipe again to jog your memory is a huge time saver when you're trying to get dinner on the table with as little effort as possible.

The other thing that takes little effort but can save a lot of time is keeping simple notes on what is in your freezer at any given time. I like to keep a running list in the Notes app on my phone, but a whiteboard on your fridge is also an easy way to do it. That way, when you are thinking about what you want to eat, you don't have to sift through piles of freezer food to come to a decision (or, even worse, leave the freezer door open longer than you should while you stand there considering your options). You can easily add and subtract dishes without a lot of effort and you'll always be able to plan ahead. So, keep a Sharpie on hand and never get lost in your freezer again.

freezer doesn't mean forever

As much as I would like to believe that our freezer truly leaves something frozen in time, it would be much more accurate to call it a delayer than a freezer. All food has a shelf life. When we leave it on the counter, we usually have a few hours or days to taste it at perfection. With a refrigerator, we delay that decay and buy ourselves another few days or weeks. With the freezer, we are extending that time into months and even years. It is hugely beneficial, but it is not forever.

That's not to say that it will become unsafe. Food that has been frozen longer than its ideal time is still edible and might still taste reasonably good, but it will start to lose flavor and texture as time goes on. If you want an overall rule of thumb, I try to use everything in my freezer within six months. Raw meats tend to last a bit longer, but ground meats and cooked meats don't stay good as long. Leaner fish like cod or flounder can hang out longer than six months but fattier varieties like salmon or tuna probably should be used a bit earlier.

Is there ever a time when you should throw something out? Not necessarily. If you packed it properly (by cooling it first, then keeping it in a nonporous, airtight container), most frozen foods should last longer than a lot of recommended timelines. Your tolerance for taste and texture is really your guide, and there are no wrong answers, but there are some organizational tips that will help you keep foods from languishing at the back of your freezer for years at a time.

To take a cue from retailers and restaurants, practice FIFO, or First In, First Out. When you put something new into the freezer, try to store it at the back, and move the older items to the front. When something goes out of sight it can go out of mind, so a little placement strategy can go a long way.

Also try to practice good freezer habits that will keep food at as consistent a temperature as possible. Don't store anything long-term in the freezer door because it can be warmer and is constantly susceptible to fluctuating temperatures. Remember that every time you open the door, you are shifting the temperature slightly, so try and have a plan and get in and out as quickly as you can. If you really want to invest in your freezer, I suggest getting a chest freezer, which tends to get opened less and is better at reducing heat coming in (because warm air rises). But a major word of warning here: the basement freezer that is often used as an excuse not to throw food away (just to have it sit frozen for five years) is not the best usage of extra freezer space!

don't be afraid to cook straight from frozen

The beauty of properly portioned meals is that, more often than not, you can cook them straight from frozen. As long as the food cooks evenly, there is no added benefit to planning ahead and defrosting. For the most part, I am a big fan of the speed of the microwave. Almost any recipe that stirs can use the microwave because the stirring allows for even cooking (as opposed to an item that can't stir, which cooks much faster on the outside than the inside). Soups, pastas, and most one-pot meals and sides can all easily get thrown in the microwave for a minute or two at a time, with stirring in between, and come out faster than and just as even as oven-cooked foods.

The oven works great for items that need crispness, can't be stirred, or need a longer cooking time. Baked items like cookies and scones, meats, and fish that need specific temperatures and appetizers can be taken straight from the freezer and popped into the oven.

And, of course, for anything fried, the freezer actually often enhances the cooking. Crab cakes, artichoke poppers, and potato pancakes all can achieve a golden exterior and a soft interior when they are cooked from frozen.

But what about when you want to defrost? Unlike from-frozen cooking there really is no shortcut to a proper defrost. Try to defrost overnight in the fridge if you can—avoid defrosting on the counter or in warm water because you might spoil the food and allow for bacteria to grow. If you want to shave a little time off, you can put a frozen item in a fully sealed plastic bag, then submerge it in cool water. Once defrosted, try to cook everything within one day.

And remember, the longer something has sat in the freezer, the more dulled the flavors will be. If you packed it and froze it properly, the losses will be more minimal, but time will always have an effect. You may need to add a bit more salt or seasoning to bring it back to life if you've left something in the freezer for a few months.

single freezer items

The freezer is great for full meals, but it also merits consideration for time-saving single ingredients. How often have you wished you had already chopped up some garlic or ginger or herbs, but you didn't have time to do it in that moment? With the freezer, you can have that. Grab an ice cube tray (preferably silicone), add some minced garlic in with olive oil, and freeze. Then, when you need a bit of garlic in a dish, just throw the cube straight into the pan. It is barely any extra effort in the moment—after all, we often have more chives or parsley than our recipe needs, and it can go bad just sitting in the fridge. These kinds of delicate items really do need to be stored in some oil (or even water), but otherwise they take to the freezer perfectly. When it comes time to quickly add it in, you will thank your past self.

Extra amounts of sauces or items like lemon juice that you might otherwise stick in the fridge to be forgotten about can also get the same treatment and go straight in an ice cube tray. You can even freeze cubes of the last dregs of your wine and coffee to be used in your cooking later. If you freeze it, you at least won't have to use it too quickly.

Beyond little flavor boosters, you can also freeze your fruits and vegetables at their peak and use them later. Anything that doesn't have too high of a moisture content will freeze beautifully on its own. Vegetables with very little water like peppers, onions, and corn can go straight into the freezer if you don't have the time or energy to blanch them. Most green vegetables such as peas, broccoli, green beans, kale, and Brussels sprouts need to be blanched or boiled for a few minutes first.

Why blanch? Because the enzymes that live in most vegetables are also what cause them to deteriorate over time. By quickly blanching, you inactivate those enzymes and help the vegetables maintain their freshness while frozen. That's why you will often see frozen vegetables advertised as being frozen right after they are harvested. By blanching

and freezing them immediately, you can really capture the peak of the season, a quality that can make frozen vegetables taste fresher than if they've sat in a truck, then in storage, then in a grocery store for days and days.

Place your vegetables in boiling water for two to three minutes (the heartier the vegetable, the longer the blanch). Immediately move them into an ice bath, then dry them completely. Don't skimp on the drying—any moisture will keep your veggies from staying in top shape. You can either cut and prep them or leave them whole. If you have the time, try to freeze on parchment paper on a sheet pan in a single layer, then place the already frozen vegetables into a bag for later.

If you have the desire to compost but you've never wanted it to take over your kitchen, freeze your food scraps! They'll be ready for compost day without anyone noticing. The freezer is truly magic—it can hold a whole meal and so much more.

appetizers

pigs in a flavor blanket

There are few things that a group will eat more rapidly than pigs in a blanket. But I thought it was about time we took the classic version up a notch. While it's always good to have some mustard or ketchup on hand to dip, this version tries to reduce the need for extra condiments. With a flavorful mixture inside, this might be the perfect bite to serve at a party (or to pop in the oven on a night when you just want a few for yourself).

Serving: 18 pigs in a flavor blanket

Ingredients
2 tablespoons mustard

2 tablespoons soy sauce

3 garlic cloves, minced

2 sheets (approximately 1 pound) puff pastry, thawed

1 (12-ounce) package hot dogs, patted dry

In a small bowl combine the mustard, soy sauce, and garlic. Roll out your pastry sheet and cut it into 3-inch squares. Then, cut each square diagonally in half. Brush the triangles with the mustard mixture. Cut the hot dogs into smaller pieces and wrap the puff pastry around them. Place on a sheet pan lined with parchment paper. Put them in the freezer until frozen, then move them to a freezer-safe container or plastic bag.

When you are ready to cook, preheat the oven to 400°F. Place the pigs on a lined sheet pan and put in the oven. Bake for 25 to 30 minutes or until the tops are golden and the insides are cooked.

brie and apple puffs

Brie and apple is a classic combination, but this version takes them over to the savory side with a bit of balsamic vinegar and salt. Don't worry about freezing blocks of cheese—once they go in the oven, they melt the same as their unfrozen counterparts. This recipe will work with any apple but the more flavor you start with the more flavor you'll end up with, so try to get sweet apples like Honeycrisp, Braeburn, or Pink Lady. This is a simple appetizer to have on hand in case you need to throw something in the oven that will please a whole crowd.

. . . .

Serving: 18 brie and apple puffs

Ingredients
2 sheets (approximately 1 pound) puff pastry, thawed
2 tablespoons balsamic vinegar
1 cup (approximately 1 whole) chopped apple
⅓ pound brie
½ teaspoon salt

Cut the puff pastry sheets into squares that are approximately 3" x 3." Brush the dough with the balsamic vinegar. In the center of each square place a small amount of apple and a small slice of brie. The apples and brie should be evenly distributed across each square. Sprinkle the salt evenly across the dough. Then wrap the dough around to close the apple and brie inside, like the shape of a dumpling, with the corners all coming up to the center. Make sure to really pinch the corners into place or they will come apart while baking (but if they come apart that's fine, too!). Place the filled dough onto a sheet pan lined with parchment paper and place in the freezer. When they are completely frozen, you can place them into a freezer-safe container or bag.

When you are ready to serve, preheat the oven to 375°F. Put the "pigs" onto a sheet pan lined with parchment paper. Bake for 18 to 20 minutes, or until the puff pastry is golden and the center has cooked.

blt mini pizzas

Sometimes two great ideas combine for an even better one. Topping the perfection of pizza with the classic bacon-lettuce-tomato trifecta is a scenario where you can't really lose. It's easy; it's a crowd-pleaser; and it cooks from frozen almost exactly the same as it does fresh. Do I even need to say more?

Serving: 18–24 small pizzas

Ingredients

2 pounds (32 ounces) pizza dough

1 cup tomato sauce

Dash salt

1 cup chopped arugula, packed

½ pound (8 ounces) regular or thinly sliced bacon

1 cup grated Parmesan cheese

Preheat the oven to 400°F. Cut the pizza dough into 18 to 24 small pieces (depending on how large you would like your pizzas), then roll each piece into a small disc. Place the dough on a parchment-lined sheet pan and put in the oven for 6 minutes. Remove and allow to cool.

On top of each piece of dough place a dollop of tomato sauce, then smooth it out, being careful not to go over the edge. Add a dash of salt, then a healthy amount of arugula (it will dramatically shrink down as it cooks), then bacon, then cheese.

If You Are Eating Now

Keep the preheated oven at 400°F and keep out your parchment-lined sheet pan. Put the mini pizzas on top of the sheet pan. Place in the oven for 10 to 15 minutes, or until the pizza is cooked to your preference (your bacon can be more or less cooked; the crust can be crispy or doughy). Remove and allow to cool before serving.

If You Are Freezing for Later

Place the mini pizzas on a sheet pan in the freezer and allow the pizzas to freeze for at least 1 hour. When they are frozen, stack the mini pizzas in between parchment paper, then place them all in a freezer-safe container or resealable plastic bag. Place in the freezer.

When you are ready to cook, preheat the oven to 400°F. Place the pizza (or pizzas) on a parchment-lined sheet pan. Place in the oven for approximately 15 minutes, or until the pizza is cooked to your preference. Remove from the oven and allow to cool before serving.

mashed potato meatballs

I'm not always a fan of mashups, but this takes the idea of Shepherd's Pie—a ground lamb casserole with mashed potatoes on top—and puts it into a delightful appetizer form. Not only do you have a flavorful combination, but the mashed potatoes actually add a lightness compared to a standard meatball. These make for fluffy little appetizer balls, or you can use them on pasta as an entrée.

Serving: 18–20 mashed potato meatballs

Ingredients
1 russet potato, peeled and chopped
1 tablespoon butter
3 tablespoons milk
1 pound ground lamb
4 garlic cloves, minced
¼ cup chopped scallions
1½ teaspoons salt

In a pot of salted boiling water, add the potato and cook for 10 minutes or until fully cooked. Drain and add back into the pot with the butter and milk. Mash until it forms mashed potatoes and allow to cool completely.

Once the potatoes are cooled add in the lamb, garlic, scallions, and salt. Stir to fully combine. Line a sheet pan with parchment paper. Roll the meat into small balls, about the size of a golf ball, and place in rows on the pan.

If You Are Eating Now
Preheat the oven to 400°F. Place the meatballs in the oven for 15 to 20 minutes, turning them over halfway through. If they haven't browned to your liking you can broil them for the last minute. Serve hot, either on their own or with a gravy of your choosing.

If You Are Freezing for Later
Place the entire sheet pan in the freezer and allow the meatballs to completely freeze. Once they are frozen (after at least an hour, but not more than 5 hours), move them into a freezer-safe container or bag.

When you are ready to cook, preheat your oven to 400°F. Place the meatballs on a lined sheet pan and put them in the oven for 30 minutes, turning once (if you want to brown them more, broil them for 1 minute at the end). Serve hot, either on their own or with a gravy of your choosing.

········· a cheese puff ·········
by any other name

I have always loved gougeres. They are basically just a cheese puff with a better name. This particular version is perfect for the freezer because it uses only Parmesan, which is a drier cheese, so they end up crisp and light as air. Keep them small—you can use a round tablespoon measure to keep them even. It's the perfect snack to always have on hand in the freezer.

Serving: 30–35 cheese puffs by any other name

Ingredients
1 cup water
8 tablespoons (1 stick) unsalted butter
½ teaspoon salt
1 cup all-purpose flour
5 large eggs
2 cups grated Parmesan cheese

Line a sheet pan with parchment paper. Combine the water, butter, and salt in a saucepan and bring to a boil over high heat. Turn the heat to low and immediately add the flour, whisking into the liquid. You want to stir quickly and long enough for the dough to get drier and much smoother; a bit of starch on the bottom is totally fine. A minute or two should be enough. Transfer to the bowl of a mixer and allow to cool for a few minutes. Then add the eggs slowly as the dough mixes (if you don't have a stand mixer, you can use a hand mixer on a low setting). The eggs should be fully mixed in and incorporated. Then add the cheese and fully incorporate that; the dough should be sticky but manageable. Scoop out the dough into approximately 1-tablespoon balls and place them on the parchment-lined sheet pan.

If You Are Eating Now
Preheat the oven to 450°F. Put the gougeres in the oven and immediately turn it down to 350°F. Bake for 25 to 30 minutes, rotating the pan once in the middle. They should be golden and puffy when cooked.

If You Are Freezing for Later
Place the sheet pan in the freezer. After an hour (or whenever they are fully frozen), place the gougeres into a resealable freezer-safe bag, removing as much air as possible. When ready to bake, preheat the oven to 450°F. Place the gougeres on a parchment-lined sheet pan. Put them in the oven and immediately turn the temperature down to 350°F. Bake for 27 to 32 minutes, rotating the pan once in the middle. They should be golden and puffy when cooked.

artichoke poppers

This recipe is all about speed: the speed of making the poppers and the speed at which they leave the plate once you put them in front of a group. This is one of those back-pocket recipes that doesn't taste as simple as its preparation is. The strong flavors of artichoke and goat cheese can still shine through the glorious extra layer of crispiness you get from frying. They make perfect appetizers or can be used as toppers for salads and grain bowls.

. . . .

Serving: 20–30 artichoke poppers

Ingredients
2 (14-ounce) cans artichoke hearts (or 3 cups)

1 egg

1 cup (6 ounces) goat cheese

1 teaspoon salt, plus more for serving

¾ cup flour

Canola oil for frying

Blend the artichoke hearts until they are mostly smooth. In a bowl combine the artichoke hearts with the egg, goat cheese, salt, and flour. On a parchment-lined sheet pan, scoop the mixture into balls (a bit smaller than a golf ball). It's okay that they don't stay in a perfect shape; the mixture firms up once it freezes. Place the pan in the freezer and leave until the balls have hardened, at least 2 hours. If you aren't cooking them that day, once they are hard you can take them off the pan and place all the balls in a resealable freezer-safe container or plastic bag.

When you are ready to cook, heat a pot of canola oil. Make sure there is enough oil to submerge as many balls as you want to cook. Heat the oil until it is 330°F to 350°F. If you don't have a thermometer you can test with a wooden spoon or chopstick. The oil is hot enough if bubbles form around the spoon or chopstick. You don't want it to be boiling or too bubbly here; if it is too hot the outside will cook before the frozen part. But you also don't want it to be too cool or the inside will get mushy, so try to always check the temperature.

Put the balls in the oil (the temperature will go down if you are making the whole batch so check to make sure it doesn't get too cold or too hot). Cook for approximately 4 to 7 minutes; you want them to be a golden-brown color. Taste test at least one or two to make sure they are fully cooked. They may take a bit longer if there are more balls. Remove from the oil and place on a paper towel. Sprinkle with additional salt while they are hot. Let cool for a moment, then serve.

tomato-mozzarella risotto balls

Any appetizer that you can make ahead, then cook straight from frozen is a multi-tasker's dream. And these risotto balls will impress any guests. It might be a little more time-consuming up front, but you make them in a big batch so that they are always ready to go when a hearty appetizer is needed. You can even keep a few extra and make them as a weeknight meal. This recipe is based on an Italian dish called arancini, which takes risotto and turns it into a golden fried confection. There's a lot of flavor in this version. The tomato sauce and cheese give a familiarity while also packing punch. Make sure to toast the risotto for longer than you might think—it adds a depth of flavor that makes it worth the time. And the basics stay the same even if you want to substitute flavors or find a use for extra leftover risotto. It's a perfect mouthful straight from the freezer.

Serving: 50–60 tomato-mozzarella risotto balls

Ingredients
8 tablespoons (1 stick) butter
32 ounces carnaroli or arborio rice
6–8 cups chicken or vegetable stock
2 cups tomato sauce or puree
1 cup finely chopped fresh basil
1 cup finely grated Parmesan cheese
Dash salt to taste, plus more for serving
4 eggs, beaten
½ cup finely diced mozzarella
2–3 cups Panko or fine bread crumbs
Canola oil for frying

Melt the butter in a wide-rimmed saucepan on medium heat. Add the rice and stir together. Cook the rice with the butter, stirring frequently, until the rice starts to toast a bit, approximately 5 minutes. Add the stock 1 cup at a time, stirring frequently. The stock should simmer but never boil. Allow at least 3 cups to soak in for at least 5 minutes of cook time before adding the tomato sauce. Let it cook, stir, and keep adding more chicken stock until the rice is almost done. It should be edible but still al dente. For exact cooking time, look at your particular rice brand's packaging. Usually, risotto takes approximately 15 to 25 minutes in total, but always keep tasting and checking. When it reaches this point, remove it from the stove and add in the basil, Parmesan, and salt. Stir vigorously until combined. Remember, you can always add more salt if needed, but you can't take it away. Taste as you add.

Set the pan aside to fully cool. If you want to cool it faster, you can spread it on a sheet pan.

When the risotto is completely cooled, add in the eggs, and fully incorporate. Place parchment paper on a sheet pan (you may need two pans depending on the size of your pans). Roll the risotto into small balls no bigger than a golf ball (if they are too big, they will not cook properly from frozen). Use your finger to make an indent in the ball, then add a small piece of mozzarella inside. Roll to close up the hole, then dredge in the bread crumbs. Set aside onto the sheet pan and repeat until all the risotto is rolled. Place the sheet pan in the freezer and allow the balls to fully freeze for at least 2 hours (but you can leave them for up to 12 if you need to). Once they are frozen, place them in a resealable freezer-safe plastic bag (you can include the parchment paper if you want an extra layer of freezer protection).

When you are ready to cook, heat a pot of canola oil. Make sure there is enough oil to submerge as many balls as you want to cook. Heat the oil until it is 330°F to 350°F. If you don't have a thermometer you can test with a wooden spoon or chopstick. The oil is hot enough if bubbles form around the spoon or chopstick. You don't want it to be boiling or too bubbly here; if it is too hot the outside will cook before the frozen part. But you also don't want it to be too cool or the inside will get mushy, so try to always check the temperature.

Put the balls in the oil (the temperature will go down if you are making the whole batch so check to make sure it doesn't get too cold or too hot). Cook for approximately 7 to 8 minutes; you want them to be a golden-brown color. Taste test at least one or two to make sure they are fully cooked. They may take a bit longer if there are more balls. Remove from the oil and place on a paper towel. Sprinkle with additional salt while they are hot. Let cool for a moment, then serve.

chapter 3

soups

beef stew with a twist

When I was a little kid, I used to make myself canned chunky beef stew and add in blueberries. In the rare instance that I could get someone to try it, they were always surprised by how the sweet tartness of blueberries melded so well with the homey goodness of beef stew. So, don't think of this as blueberry and beef stew, but instead as beef stew with a delightful twist.

Serving: 6–8

Ingredients

1 tablespoon extra-virgin olive oil

Dash salt and pepper

3–4 pounds whole boneless beef chuck roast, halved

1 tablespoon apple cider vinegar

1 large white onion, diced

4 medium carrots, diced

1½ pounds (24 ounces) small potatoes, diced

¼ cup cornstarch

1 tablespoon anchovy paste

2 tablespoons Worcestershire sauce

2 tablespoons tomato paste

1½ cups blueberries, divided

3 cups chicken or beef stock

2 cups frozen peas

Preheat the oven to 300°F. Place a large Dutch oven or pan large enough for all ingredients on medium-high heat with the olive oil. Add salt and pepper on all sides of the chuck roast, then place in the pan. Cook for 8 to 10 minutes, rotating every few minutes to allow another side to brown. When all sides are brown, set aside to cool. Deglaze the pan by adding in the apple cider vinegar—make sure to scrape the brown bits from the bottom. Add in the onion and cook for 5 minutes. Add in the carrots and potatoes and cook for 5 additional minutes. While the vegetables are cooking, cut the chuck roast into 1-inch cubes. In a small bowl combine the cornstarch, anchovy paste, Worcestershire sauce, and tomato paste. Take half of the vegetable mixture out of the pot and set it to the side. Add the combined sauces, ½ cup blueberries, and stock into the pot along with the chuck roast. Stir together and bring to a simmer. Put the pot in the oven, covered, for 1 hour. Add the remaining vegetables back into the pot along with another ½ cup blueberries. Place back in the oven for another hour.

If You Are Eating Now

Remove from the oven and add the peas and remaining blueberries. If the sauce is a bit thin you can put the pot back on the stove top for a few minutes and cook until it has reduced to your liking. Serve hot.

If You Are Freezing for Later

Remove the pot from the oven and allow it to completely cool down. Add the frozen peas and the blueberries. Place the stew into freezer-safe containers or bags in individual servings and put them into the freezer. When you are ready to eat, reheat the stew in the microwave a minute or two at a time, stirring in between, until hot.

pork chili

Any book about freezer food has to include a chili—it's like the patron saint of food that gets even more delicious the longer it sits. But while there are many takes on chili, I only want to deal with the ones that are as easy to make as they are to heat up. I love a good, braised meat, but sometimes the amount of time is just not worth it. While you see a lot of pork chilis with pulled pork, this version mercifully cuts down the time dramatically without sacrificing the flavor. By browning the ground pork, adding spices like cumin and chili powder, and finishing with the hoppy effervescence of beer, you get complex flavors without the complex timing. Eat some now and save some for later—both times you'll be glad to have something easy up your sleeve.

Serving: 6–8

Ingredients
2 large yellow onions, diced
Dash olive oil
Dash salt + 2 teaspoons, divided
2 pounds ground pork
4 garlic cloves, minced
1 teaspoon cumin
1 teaspoon chili powder
1 (28-ounce) can diced tomatoes
2 (15-ounce) cans kidney beans
1 (12-ounce) can beer

In a large stockpot on medium-high heat, cook the yellow onions with olive oil and a dash of salt for 5 to 7 minutes, or until they begin to soften. Add the pork, garlic, cumin, and chili powder and cook for another 5 to 8 minutes, or until the pork has browned a bit. Drain the tomatoes and kidney beans and reserve their liquid if you like a soupier chili. Add the tomatoes, kidney beans and the beer to the pot. Bring to a low boil and cook for 20 minutes, uncovered, stirring occasionally. If you want the chili to have a soupier consistency, you can add back in some of the reserved tomato and bean liquid.

If You Are Eating Now
Cook an additional 5 minutes or longer if you want to allow more time to thicken, then add remaining salt. Add more salt if needed. Serve hot.

If You Are Freezing for Later
Let the chili cool down completely, then add remaining salt. Add more salt if needed. Separate the chili into individual servings in freezer-safe containers or freezer bags (the best containers are those that can go straight from the fridge to the microwave, since bags can get messy).

When you are ready to eat, place the chili in the microwave and cook 1 minute at a time, stirring in between, until hot.

······· corn soup with ·········
chickpeas and coconut

My sister always notices when I use curry powder in a recipe because it isn't her favorite, but this dish got her on my side. A subtle hint of it, along with crowd-pleasers like coconut milk, ginger, and lime, can take a dish with a lot of flavors and meld them seamlessly into something that everyone will agree on. And it's one of the few soups that can go into the freezer and still feel bright when it comes out.

Serving: 8–10

Ingredients
1 tablespoon extra-virgin olive oil
4 garlic cloves
1 yellow onion, chopped
8 ears corn
2 (13.5-ounce) cans coconut milk
5 cups water
2 tablespoons ginger, peeled and chopped
Juice of 3 limes
2 teaspoons curry powder
²/₃ cup finely chopped parsley
2 (15-ounce) cans chickpeas, drained and rinsed
Dash salt

Place a large pot on medium-high heat. Add the olive oil, garlic, and onion. Sauté for 5 to 7 minutes until the onion starts to brown a bit and become translucent. While the onion is cooking, cut the corn off the ears of corn. Add the coconut milk, water, ginger, lime juice, and curry powder to the pot along with the ears of corn and half the corn. Bring to a low simmer, cover, and cook for 20 minutes. When the soup is done simmering, remove the ears of corn. Add the liquid into a blender or use an immersion blender to blend the contents of the soup.

If You Are Eating Now
Add in the rest of the corn, parsley, chickpeas, and salt to taste. (Add in a little salt as you go, so as not to oversalt, but don't skimp either. This should have lots of flavor! I like at least 1 teaspoon.) Cook the soup for another 2 to 3 minutes, then serve hot.

If You Are Freezing for Later
Let the liquid cool down to room temperature. Add in the additional corn, parsley, chickpeas, and salt (at least 1 teaspoon). Place the soup in small freezer containers or heavy-duty freezer bags. When you are ready to eat, this soup can be reheated from frozen either in a microwave or on the stove top. In the microwave, cook in 1-minute increments, stirring as you go. On the stove, place on medium heat and stir frequently—you do not want the block of soup in frozen form to burn on the bottom. Taste to make sure you have enough salt (sometimes soups can benefit from a bit more salt after they've been frozen) and serve hot.

fired-up tomato soup

Tomato is among the most comforting soups. But this twist on the classic adds a depth that also lends well to freezing. I find that if typical tomato soups rely too heavily on the freshness of the main ingredient and the herbs that go along with it, freezing can detract from that freshness. But a soup where the tomatoes are heavily cooked and have another layer of flavor can easily be frozen. And it's versatile—throw in some chicken you already cooked or pasta you have lying around or serve it alongside a good piece of fresh bread with some Parmesan sprinkled on top.

Serving: 6–8

Ingredients
10 (3–4 pounds) medium tomatoes
2 medium onions, roughly chopped
4 large garlic cloves
Drizzle extra-virgin olive oil
½ cup chopped basil
4 cups vegetable or chicken stock
   (or water in a pinch)
Dash salt

Preheat oven to 450°F. Line a sheet pan with aluminum foil and place the tomatoes, onions, and garlic cloves on it. Drizzle with olive oil to coat and place the pan in the oven. Cook for 30 to 40 minutes (the timing will depend on the size of your tomatoes). When the tomatoes are very soft and have started to brown, turn the broiler on and let the vegetables cook until they have blackened a bit, approximately 3 to 5 minutes.

Remove the pan from the oven and put the tomatoes, onions, and garlic in a large pot or blender with the basil and stock or water. Then, use an immersion blender (or just turn on your blender) until the mixture is smooth. Taste and add a heavy dash of salt (at minimum 1 teaspoon, but then add more salt to your preference).

If You Are Eating Now
Place or keep the soup in a pot on medium-high heat. Cook, stirring occasionally, until the soup has reached the desired temperature. Serve hot.

If You Are Freezing for Later

Place the soup into freezer-safe containers or resealable freezer bags. The best containers are those that can go straight from the fridge to the microwave, since bags can get messy. Make sure to divide the soup enough so that it is in individual servings—the last thing you want is a giant block of 8 servings of soup when you only need a single bowl. Put the soup in the freezer.

When you are ready to eat, remove the soup from its packaging. You can microwave it in a bowl for 1 minute at a time, stirring until it reaches the desired heat and consistency. Or you can place it in a pot and heat on medium-high heat, stirring consistently.

Note: this recipe does not yield as much as other soups in this book because the ingredients fit on a single sheet pan. If you'd like to double (or triple) this recipe, follow the same instructions but make sure to give each sheet pan separate time under the broiler. The charring time is key.

mint pea soup with a bite

Mint pea soup is a classic, but I have always felt that it could be turned up a notch. The simplicity of the pea is incredible when you have fresh ones in the spring, but for most of the year (and for those of us who don't have the time to shuck them), we are creating a soup to showcase an ingredient that isn't at its peak. This recipe adds that kick in just the slightest of ways. By using a touch of red onion and scallions, you change the soup's entire dynamic. And while it can be served hot, it is equally as good cold or at room temperature. This is a dynamic little version of a soup that will be perfect for any season, despite its seemingly seasonal main ingredient.

Serving: 8–10

Ingredients
1 tablespoon extra-virgin olive oil
1 large yellow onion, diced
4 garlic cloves, minced
6 cups vegetable or chicken stock
2 (10-ounce) packages frozen peas
Juice of ½ lemon
½ cup chopped mint
2 teaspoons salt
¼ cup diced scallions
¼ cup very finely diced red onion
½ cup sour cream (optional)

Place a large pot on medium-high heat and add the olive oil, yellow onion, and garlic. Cook for 5 to 7 minutes, or until the onion starts to soften and become translucent. Add the stock and bring to a boil. Add 4 cups of peas (reserving 1 cup for later) and cook for 1 minute. Remove from the heat, add lemon and mint, and blend using a blender or immersion blender. Add the remaining peas and the salt. Allow the soup to cool down to room temperature, then add the scallions and red onion.

If You Are Eating Now
If you want to serve it hot, you can bring it back up to your desired temperature but serve immediately so that the scallions and onion don't cook too much. If you want to serve it at room temperature, just serve as is. You can also refrigerate it and serve it cold. In any of these scenarios you can place a small dollop of sour cream on top if you desire.

If You Are Freezing for Later
Divide the soup into single-serving freezer containers (or even freezer-safe resealable bags) and place in the freezer. To eat cold, allow the soup to defrost overnight in the fridge. To eat hot, cook it in a microwave 1 minute at a time until it comes to temperature.

roasted carrot and ginger soup

My mother-in-law introduced me to the deliciously simple combination of carrot and ginger soup because my husband is basically a ginger fanatic. But it works even for those who aren't inhaling ginger on a regular basis. The earthy nature of roasted carrots is the perfect background for the zing of ginger.

Serving: 8

Ingredients

3 pounds (9–12 medium-sized) carrots
1 large yellow onion, roughly diced
Drizzle extra-virgin olive oil
4 garlic cloves
2 tablespoons peeled and minced ginger
6 cups vegetable broth, plus more as needed
1 teaspoon ground coriander
¼ cup sour cream
1 teaspoon salt, plus more as needed
Parsley (optional)

Preheat the oven to 450°F. Place the carrots and onions on an oiled sheet pan. Drizzle with a bit more olive oil and roll the carrots around until they are covered. Roast them for 40 to 50 minutes, making sure to turn halfway through. The cook time really depends on the size of your carrots, so check on them to be sure. They are done when they are caramelized on all sides and tender throughout. For those last 10 minutes add the garlic on top. Once the carrots and onions are ready, add them to a pot or into your blender along with the ginger, 2 cups vegetable broth, and coriander. Blend with an immersion blender or blender to combine. Add the remaining broth and sour cream and blend again until smooth. Add salt.

If You Are Eating Now

Cook the soup on medium heat for approximately 5 minutes to bring to a hot temperature. Add fresh parsley on top if you'd like.

If You Are Freezing for Later

Divide the soup into individual servings into freezer-safe bowls or resealable freezer bags (the best containers are those that can go straight from the fridge to the microwave, since bags can get messy). Put them in the freezer. When you are ready to eat, remove the soup from the bowl or bag. You can reheat either in the microwave or on the stove top. For the microwave, place the soup in a microwave-safe bowl and microwave for 1 minute at a time, stirring in between, until it is hot. For the stove top, you can put the soup in a pot on medium-high heat and stir until it reaches the desired temperature. You can add a small amount of water to help reconstitute if needed. Add fresh parsley on top if you'd like.

onion-tastic soup

Sometimes a basic name doesn't do justice to a recipe. This recipe takes plain old onion soup to the next level. The long cooking time allows the onions to get to their deepest flavors and the result is electrifying. It's also devilishly easy: 5 ingredients (including salt and water) thrown in a pot. That's pretty much it. Make it when you have some time to stir occasionally and you'll have a soup that will make you look at onions with a whole new level of respect.

Serving: 6

Ingredients

5 medium yellow onions, diced
6 large garlic cloves, minced
½ cup extra-virgin olive oil
1 teaspoon salt, plus more as needed

Preheat the oven to 400°F. In a large Dutch oven or heavy bottomed pot, add the onions, garlic, olive oil, and salt. Stir a bit to combine. Cover and place in the oven. Allow the onions to cook for at least 2 hours, stirring every 20 minutes or so (especially toward the end, to make sure the onions are caramelizing but not getting stuck to the bottom). Remove from the oven and add just enough water to meet your preferred soup consistency. (About 4 cups does it for me.) Taste, add more salt as needed, and serve.

If You Are Freezing for Later

Let the soup cool down completely. Place in freezer-safe containers, taking care to portion it out so the soup isn't in a giant block (the best containers are those that can go straight from the fridge to the microwave, since bags can get messy). You can microwave from frozen, 1 minute at a time, stirring in between. Serve hot.

lentil and veggie soup

Lentil soup can be a dull, flavorless option that feels like a dietary punishment, or it can be a vibrant vegetarian dream. This recipe tries to keep enough tricks in its pocket so that it stays firmly in the dreamy category. First, it uses red and green lentils so that there are diverging textures. Second, the diced tomatoes give a bit of extra substance. And last, I use cinnamon. This memorable soup also works out well when you want to stay on the healthier side and have some frozen for a rainy day.

Serving: 8–10

Ingredients
2 tablespoons extra-virgin olive oil
2 medium yellow onions, finely diced
2 carrots, peeled and finely chopped
6 garlic cloves, minced
2 teaspoons curry powder
1 teaspoon cinnamon
Juice of 1 lemon
2 (28-ounce) cans diced tomatoes
2 cups green or brown lentils
2 cups red lentils
6 cups vegetable broth
2 teaspoons salt, plus more as needed
3 cups chopped lacinato kale, center stalks
   removed

Place a large pot or Dutch oven on medium-high heat. Add the olive oil, onions, and carrots and cook for 5 minutes or until the onions have begun to soften (try not to stir too much, so that they brown a bit on the bottom). Add the garlic, curry powder, cinnamon, and lemon juice. Cook for an additional minute. Add in the diced tomatoes, lentils, broth, and salt. Raise the heat to get the mixture to just come to a boil, then reduce the heat to a simmer. Cook 25 to 30 minutes or until the lentils have softened, but still have a touch of a bite.

If You Are Eating Now
Add the kale and cook an additional 5 minutes. Taste for whether you need a bit more salt, then serve.

If You Are Freezing for Later
Add the kale and leave the pot open to fully cool down. Once the soup has come to room temperature, separate it into servings in freezer-safe containers or freezer bags. When you are ready to serve, you can put the soup back in a pot on the stove or in a microwave. Just make sure to stir consistently until it comes to temperature. You can always add a bit more water if needed to reconstitute. If you feel like the flavors have been dulled a bit by the freezer, add another dash of curry powder and cinnamon.

sunchoke soup

Sunchokes, also known as Jerusalem artichokes, don't look like much on the surface—mostly like gnarled, brown carrots. But inside they are packed with an earthy, addictive flavor that needs little else to make them shine. If you have an ingredient that everyone isn't as familiar with, sometimes it is enough to be amazing on its own, so this recipe doubles down and keeps it light. Unlike some other recipes with sunchokes, this one doesn't necessitate peeling. I think it adds a lot of flavor and, more importantly, saves a lot time. Keep the skin, add a few other ingredients, and you're good to go.

Serving: 10–12

Ingredients

2 tablespoons extra-virgin olive oil, plus more
  as needed
2 large onions, diced
6 garlic cloves
2 tablespoons minced ginger
3 pounds sunchokes, scrubbed and roughly
  diced
10 cups water
1 teaspoon salt, plus more as needed

Put the olive oil and onions in a large pot on medium-high heat. Cook, without stirring too much, until the onions have softened and become a bit translucent, about 5 to 7 minutes. Add the garlic and ginger (add more olive oil as needed) and cook an additional 2 minutes. Add the sunchokes and water. Bring to a boil, add the salt, then reduce the heat. Let the soup cook for 30 minutes until the sunchokes have completely softened (if they have not, you can always cook longer). Blend the soup fully in a blender or with a hand mixer. Taste to see if additional salt is needed. If eating now, serve hot.

If You Are Freezing for Later

Allow the soup to fully cool down. Once the soup has come to room temperature separate it into individual servings in freezer-safe containers or freezer bags (the best containers are those that can go straight from the fridge to the microwave, since bags can get messy).

When you are ready to eat, you can put the soup back in a pot on the stove or in a microwave. Just make sure to stir consistently until it comes to temperature. You can always add a bit more water if needed to reconstitute.

turmeric bean soup

The best combinations are simple and surprising. This soup delivers on both counts: it's so easy that you don't even have to drain the beans you're using, and the combination of turmeric and cardamom with a kick of ginger is so addictive you'll want to always have some in your freezer for a cold day. It's the kind of dish you can serve to guests or make a batch of for weekday lunch.

Serving: 4–6

Ingredients

1 tablespoon extra-virgin olive oil
1 large yellow onion, diced
6 garlic cloves, minced
1 tablespoon minced ginger
Dash + 1 teaspoon salt, divided
¼ teaspoon turmeric
¼ teaspoon ground cardamom
5 cups vegetable broth
1 cup green lentils
1 (15-ounce) can black beans, including the liquid
1 (15-ounce) can cannellini beans, including the liquid
Parsley (optional)

Put a pot on medium-high heat and add the olive oil, onion, garlic, ginger, and dash of salt. Cook for 10 minutes, or until the onions are soft and have begun to caramelize. Add the turmeric and cardamom, stir, and let cook for an additional minute. Then, add the vegetable broth. Bring to a boil, then reduce the heat. Add the lentils and cook for approximately 15 minutes or until they have begun to soften and are almost ready to eat. (If you like your lentils softer, feel free to cook longer, but I find that al dente texture makes them even better after time in the freezer.) Once they are cooked, add the black and cannellini beans. Taste, then add salt (depending on the beans and the broth you might need no more or alternately even a few teaspoons more). You can also add a bit more of the cardamom if you want a stronger flavor.

If You Are Eating Now
Cook for another minute, then serve hot if eating now. Add parsley on top if desired.

If You Are Freezing for Later
Allow the soup to fully cool. Separate it into servings in freezer-safe containers or freezer bags (the best containers are those that can go straight from the fridge to the microwave, since bags can get messy).

When you are ready to eat, you can defrost or cook the soup straight from frozen. If cooking on the stove top, make sure to defrost on a low temperature. In the microwave, cook in 1-minute increments, stirring as you go. Add parsley on top if desired.

.... chapter 4 ....

one-pot meals

bacony greens with beans

So many healthy one-pot meals start with some greens and some beans, but they are often lacking in the flavor department. The one-two punch of the feta and the bacon here make this dish irresistible. With only 4 ingredients and less than 15 minutes, this recipe might be the perfect weeknight solution made even easier by its ability to get thrown in the freezer to live another day.

Serving: 8

Ingredients
16 ounces bacon, chopped into small pieces
4 bunches Swiss chard, chopped
4 (15-ounce) cans navy beans, drained
1½ cups feta cheese, crumbled

Place the bacon in a pan on medium-high heat and let it cook for 2 minutes. Add the Swiss chard to the pan. Stir occasionally and let cook for 3 to 4 more minutes, or until the chard has wilted and the bacon is cooked. Add the beans and cook for an additional minute. Turn the heat off and add in the feta.

If You Are Freezing for Later
Let the mixture cool down, then separate into individual servings in freezer-safe containers or bags and place in the freezer. When ready to eat, you can heat this back up in the microwave, cooking 1 minute at a time, stirring in between.

twice-baked loaded potatoes

I always loved baked potatoes as a kid because they felt like a blank canvas. I could mix in whatever vegetables or herbs (or, let's be real—butter) I wanted. Gathering ingredients and waiting to bake a potato isn't always the simplest solution, but once the freezer gets involved, you can have the best of both worlds. This recipe is great to have on hand because all you have to do is throw it into the oven to have an entire meal. The toppings are great for adults and kids alike due to its hidden vegetables, and it packs a lot of flavor thanks to garlic, lemon, and chives. The salami doesn't hurt either, although you can leave it out if you have any vegetarians present (just be sure to add an extra dash of salt to make up for it)! Go ahead, load up your potatoes so that you later have an easy meal in a flash.

Serving: 8

Ingredients

8 large russet potatoes
2 tablespoons vegetable oil
Dash salt + 1 teaspoon salt, divided
½ cup whole milk
4 tablespoons unsalted butter, melted
2 garlic cloves, grated
1 cup finely chopped kale
1 cup frozen peas
1 cup finely grated Parmesan cheese, plus
    more as needed
Juice of ½ lemon
½ cup chopped chives
1 cup chopped salami (optional)

Preheat the oven to 400°F. Place the potatoes on a sheet pan lined with aluminum foil and rub with vegetable oil and a dash of salt. Cook for 1 hour. The potato skins should be browned, and the inside should be softened. Let them fully cool to room temperature. Slice the tops off the potatoes (but try to leave a little space at each end so it is almost like a pocket—you can eat those cut potato skins separately if you like). Spoon out as much of the potato as you can without breaking the skin and ensuring the potato won't fall apart when you stuff it back together. Place it in a bowl with the rest of the salt, milk, and butter. Mash until combined. Add the garlic, kale, peas, Parmesan cheese, lemon juice, chives, and salami if using (if not, add in another dash of salt to compensate), and combine. Spoon the mixture into the potato skins; it should rise a bit higher than the potato and that's okay.

If You Are Eating Now

Preheat the oven to 400°F. Place the potatoes on a sheet pan lined with aluminum foil and put them in the oven for 20 minutes, or until they are hot and have started to brown. Serve hot.

If You Are Freezing for Later

Wrap each potato tightly in aluminum foil and place them all in a resealable plastic freezer bag. When you are ready to cook, you can either defrost them or cook them straight from frozen. In either scenario, you can cook the potatoes on top of the aluminum foil they were already wrapped in.

(Continued on next page)

To defrost, thaw them overnight. When you are ready to cook, preheat the oven to 400°F and cook the potatoes for 20 minutes, unwrapped in their aluminum foil.

If coming straight from the freezer, preheat the oven to 400°F. Unwrap the potatoes but leave them on top of their foil. Cook for 35 to 45 minutes until soft and browning. If you are heating more than one, you may want to cook a bit on the longer side. Serve hot.

·········· lentils, carrots, and quinoa ··········
with harissa-feta dressing

This recipe packs a lot of flavor without a lot of additional effort. Harissa, a North African spicy and smoky chili paste, combined with the twin notes of feta and mint, bring a lot of dimension to a very healthy dish that has no business being as delicious as it is.

Serving: 8

Ingredients
2 cups quinoa
4 cups red lentils
⅓ cup harissa
2 cups shredded carrots
2 cups spinach
½ cup mint
2 cups feta, crumbled
Dash salt

Add 7 cups of water to a pot along with the quinoa, lentils, and harissa. Bring up to a boil and add the carrots. Reduce heat to a strong simmer and cover, stirring every few minutes.

If You Are Eating Now
After 8 or 9 minutes (or when the quinoa and lentils feel cooked but still a bit al dente) add the spinach, mint, and feta to the lentil-quinoa mixture. Cook for an additional minute or two, taste to see if you need any more salt, and serve hot.

If You Are Freezing for Later
After 8 or 9 minutes (or when the quinoa and lentils feel cooked but still a bit al dente) remove the pot from the heat and allow to cool down completely. When cooled, add the spinach, mint, and feta into the lentil-quinoa mixture. Divide into individual servings and freeze in a freezer-safe container or resealable bag. When ready to eat, microwave the individual servings 1 minute at a time, stirring in between, until hot.

·········· creamy leeks ··········
with bulgur and gouda

I believe that bulgur is one of the most underrated grains. It gets pigeonholed as being only for tabbouleh but it's really something that should be in the repertoire as much as rice or quinoa. It has a nuttier, chewier texture, which makes it a great addition to any vegetarian dishes that might feel like they need some extra heft. And because of that naturally chewy status, it holds up great in the freezer. This recipe lets bulgur shine with gentle leeks and a punch of gouda. Use it as a main for vegetarians or keep it as an extra side for a day when you don't want to make something new from scratch.

Serving: 4 as a main; 8 as a side

Ingredients
Drizzle extra-virgin olive oil
12 garlic cloves, chopped
12 leeks
Dash salt
1½ cups vegetable or chicken stock
1½ cups heavy cream
1½ cups bulgur
1 cup chopped basil
1½ cups grated Gouda (aged preferred)
Juice of 1 lemon

Place a large pan on medium-high heat with the olive oil. Add garlic to the pan. Wash and chop the leeks into bite-sized pieces, only using the white portion. Add the leeks to the pan with a dash of salt, the stock, cream, and bulgur. Bring the liquid to a low boil and cook, stirring fairly frequently. Add half the basil to the leeks.

If You Are Eating Now
After the leeks and bulgur have been cooking for about 7 to 10 minutes (and the bulgur is al dente), add the remaining basil, all the Gouda, and lemon juice. Combine and serve hot.

If You Are Freezing for Later
Let the leeks and bulgur cook for 7 to 10 minutes. The bulgur should be al dente. Remove from the heat and add the remaining basil, the Gouda, and lemon juice. Let everything fully cool down. When cool, separate into portions and place in a resealable freezer-safe bag or container and freeze.

When ready to cook, reheat in the microwave 1 minute at a time, stirring in between, until the bulgur and leeks are fully cooked and hot.

kicked-up roasted
brussels sprouts and chicken sausage

Cooking everything together in one fell swoop makes a meal feel a bit like magic. But this recipe takes it to the next level because it can also be frozen. I love the combination of sausage with Brussels sprouts because it feels like a fair match—neither overpowers the other, and both are supported by the verve of apple and sriracha. Sometimes simplicity wins, and this dish is the very definition of it.

Serving: 6–8

Ingredients
3 pounds Brussels sprouts, trimmed and halved

3 large green apples, diced

3 pounds (already cooked) chicken sausage, diced

Dash extra-virgin olive oil

Dash salt

3 tablespoons sriracha

Turn on your broiler. Toss all ingredients together in a bowl. Place half the mixture on a sheet pan with aluminum foil; spread out in a single layer. You will need to do two batches to spread the mixture thin enough; it will not cook if the pan is too crowded.

Place the mixture under the broiler for 4 to 7 minutes. You will know it is done when the Brussels and sausage have started to brown, and the Brussels are soft enough to eat but still have a crunch. Remove the first batch from the pan and repeat with the remaining mixture.

If You Are Freezing for Later
Allow the Brussels and sausage to cool down completely. Place in freezer-safe containers or bags in individual servings, then put in the freezer. When you are ready to eat, heat the mixture up 1 minute at a time, stirring in between, until it is hot.

white bean and
artichoke jumble

This dish is one of those tricky ones to categorize. It's not quite a stew because it's a little too thick. It's not a grain bowl since it has no grains. It can be a side, but it is hearty enough to be a main. I've settled on calling it a jumble, because it is a great big bowl of delicious ingredients that come together in less than 15 minutes and somehow make for a desirable, simple recipe that works as well from frozen as it does from the start. It has a lot of pantry staples, but all are healthy. And the tarragon adds a burst of freshness while the Roquefort adds its own special punch. Whatever this jumble is, it's a perfect one-pot meal for any time of year.

Serving: 8

Ingredients
4 (14-ounce) cans navy or cannellini beans, drained
4 (14-ounce) cans artichoke hearts, drained
2 (28-ounce) cans diced tomatoes
1 cup chopped tarragon
Dash salt, plus more if needed
1 cup Roquefort or other crumbly blue cheese

Put the beans, artichoke hearts, tomatoes, tarragon, and salt into a large pot. Bring to a heavy simmer for 5 minutes.

If You Are Eating Now
Add the Roquefort and stir together. Taste to see if you need any more salt. Serve hot.

If You Are Freezing for Later
Let the mixture fully cool down. Add the Roquefort and stir together. Taste to see if you need any more salt. Place in single-serving freezer-safe containers and put in the freezer. When you are ready to eat, microwave for 2 minutes at a time, stirring in between, until hot.

chana masala-ish

When I lived in India, I gained such a firm appreciation for beans and legumes as the basis for an entire meal. It felt like the ever-so-distant cousin of the beans and rice I grew up with in the South, but with an excitingly different knack for knocking flavor out of the park (especially often in the absence of meat). One dish that I loved instantly was chana masala, a chickpea-tomato dish that often boasts a dozen or more spices perfectly melding together to create a cacophony of flavors that can be served alone or over rice. I would not presume to be able to make a definitive version, but this is the homage I make at home. The classic versions feature amchoor, a dried mango powder that you can find online or at specialty markets and that make an excellent addition, but I think my non-traditional version can get you hooked enough to maybe encourage a trip to India for the real thing.

Serving: 8

Ingredients
2 large onions, diced

6 garlic cloves, diced

2 teaspoons salt, plus more as needed

2 tablespoons extra-virgin olive oil, plus more as needed

2 teaspoons turmeric powder

2 teaspoons ground cumin

2 teaspoons ground coriander

2 teaspoons curry powder

4 large tomatoes, diced

4 (16-ounce) cans chickpeas, drained

Juice of 2 limes

Place the onions and garlic in a pan on medium-high heat with a dash of salt and olive oil. Add all the spices and cook down for 5 to 7 minutes, until the onions start to look translucent. Add the tomatoes into the pan. Cook down for another 3 minutes, then add the chickpeas and lime juice.

If You Are Eating Now
Cook for another 2 to 3 minutes and serve hot.

If You Are Freezing for Later
Remove from the heat and allow to completely cool down. Freeze in individual servings in freezer-safe containers or resealable freezer bags. When you are ready to eat, heat in the microwave, 1 minute at a time, stirring in between until hot.

edamame "risotto"

I love risotto, but it is clearly not a contender for freezing. (Getting that perfect texture is hard enough right from the start.) But one night, at one of my favorite restaurants in New York, Bessou, I saw risotto in a new light. With brown rice and soy milk, they created that creamy texture with the al dente bite of a risotto, but with a bit of a flavor twist. After putting my own spin on this recipe, it became clear that it was a great contender for freezing. What you end up with is a rice dish that can stand the test of time, unlike a real risotto.

. . . .

Serving: 6–8 as a meal; 10–12 as an appetizer

Ingredients
4 cups unsweetened soy milk
1 cup vegetable broth
1 teaspoon salt, plus more as needed
Juice of 2 large lemons
3 cups brown rice
10–12 radishes, diced
2 cups grated Parmesan cheese
2 cups shelled edamame

Put the soy milk, broth, salt, and lemon juice in a medium pot and bring to a boil. Add the rice, reduce the heat, and cook for 30 to 40 minutes, covered. You'll know it's ready when it the rice is edible but just slightly underdone.

While the rice is cooking, turn the broiler on and line a sheet pan with foil. Add the radishes with a dash of salt and put them under the broiler for 2 to 5 minutes, or until they are cooked but still have a crispy bite.

. . . .

If You Are Eating Now
Add the radishes, Parmesan, and edamame to the pot with the rice and combine. Taste to see if additional salt is needed (I like up to 1 teaspoon more salt but taste as you go). Serve hot.

If You Are Freezing for Later
Allow the rice to completely cool down. Add the radishes, Parmesan, and edamame. Stir, then taste to see if additional salt is needed (I like up to 1 teaspoon more salt but taste as you go). Divide the "risotto" into individual single-serving freezer-safe containers or bags. Put into the freezer.

When you are ready to eat the "risotto" again, put each serving in the microwave for 1 or 2 minutes at a time, stirring in between. Add a little bit of water to reconstitute if it needs it.

lemon beef and broccoli

Sometimes a specific combination of two ingredients becomes so popular that they seemingly can't be combined any other way. The brown sauce used in the Americanized Chinese dish of beef and broccoli may seem like the only inevitable conclusion of that meat and vegetable duo, but these ingredients are great together for more than just that one sauce. In this recipe, a large dose of lemon and Parmesan sauce adds a bold zest to the proceedings. This dish also fares well with freezing: if you keep the broccoli crisp it won't end up wilting on the second round; chuck roast takes well to long cooking times; and the brightness of the sauce makes it all sing (even if cooked straight from frozen).

Serving: 8–10

Ingredients

3 tablespoons butter
4 pounds chuck roast
4 teaspoons salt, divided
7½ cups beef broth, divided
2 pounds broccoli, cut into small florets
3 cups short-grain brown rice
Juice of 4 lemons
¼ cup soy sauce
½ cup grated Parmesan cheese
¼ cup mayonnaise

Preheat the oven to 300°F. Place a large pot or Dutch oven on medium-high heat and add the butter. Heavily salt the chuck roast on all sides (approximately 2 teaspoons) and add it to the melted butter. Allow the roast to brown, turning occasionally, for about 3 to 4 minutes on each side. Add 2 cups beef broth and bring to a simmer. Put the top on the pot and place in the oven. Cook for 4 hours or until fully tender. Remove the beef from the pot but leave the sauce in and add the broccoli to it. Cook covered in the oven for 5 minutes. When finished, remove the broccoli from the pot and set aside with the beef to cool. The broccoli should be cooked enough to eat but still very crunchy.

Add the remaining beef stock to the pot. Place the pot back on the stove on medium-high heat until it comes to a boil. Add the rice and at least one teaspoon salt and cook according to package time (the final amount of salt will depend on your preference and the saltiness of the broth). While the rice is cooking, shred the beef into small pieces.

Combine the lemon juice, soy sauce, Parmesan, mayonnaise, and remaining teaspoon of salt. Combine the sauce, beef, and broccoli with the rice.

(Continued on next page)

If You Are Eating Now

Put everything back in the oven for 5 minutes. Serve hot.

If You Are Freezing for Later

Allow the beef and broccoli to cool completely. Split into individual portions. Make sure the beef is truly shredded and the broccoli is cut small, otherwise it won't unfreeze as uniformly. Freeze in freezer containers or resealable freezer bags.

When ready to eat, you can reheat in either the microwave or the oven. In the oven, cook at 400°F for at least 15 minutes per portion, making sure to stir every 5 minutes. In the microwave, cook for 1 or 2 minutes at a time, stirring in between.

no-scraps veggie bake

There is nothing more satisfying than making a dish without anything to clean up at the end. This veggie bake is hearty, delicious, and surreptitiously sustainable. It takes three vegetables that often have parts thrown away—fennel fronds, carrot tops, and potato skins—and allows them to cook down until they are almost melted together harmoniously. Unlike a lot of recipes in this book, this recipe is not meant to be divided into individual portions. It is a dish meant to be served as one item that has been given a lot of time to cook, but that time will be worth it for a vegetarian meal that celebrates simplicity while still packing in a ton of flavor.

Serving: 4–8

Ingredients

3 heads fennel

1 pound carrots

2 large russet potatoes

Extra-virgin olive oil for the pan

2 teaspoons salt, divided

1 cup ricotta

1 (24-ounce) jar tomato sauce

½ cup grated Parmesan cheese

Preheat the oven to 400°F. Cut the fennel bulbs from the tops and cut the bulbs into slices. Cut off the fronds (the parts that look like herbs) from the stalks and set aside. Finely chop the stalks. Remove the carrot tops from the carrots. Cut the carrots into long halves (or quarters if the carrots are particularly large). Chop the carrot tops finely. Slice the potatoes into ½-inch slices, leaving the skin on.

In a large baking dish (it can be circular or square and almost any size—it will all cook the same), spread a layer of olive oil at the bottom. Place the potatoes in rows, overlapping them to cover the entire bottom of the pan. Add a generous dash of salt to the potatoes. Spread a thin layer of ricotta on top (it can be more like dime-sized dollops if your ricotta's texture is thick), salt it, then spread a layer of tomato sauce. If your tomato sauce is not salted enough, make sure to add salt—this dish needs every layer salted! Sprinkle all of the carrot tops on top along with another dash of salt. Place a layer of the fennel slices down and give them another dash of salt. Add another layer of ricotta, then tomato sauce (and a dash of salt!). Add a layer of carrots with another dash of salt. Top with another ricotta and tomato layer (don't forget the dash

(Continued on next page)

of salt!), then add the chopped fennel stalks on top. Cover with aluminum foil and place in the oven for 60 minutes. Remove from the oven and sprinkle the fennel fronds and Parmesan on top.

If You Are Eating Now
Cook uncovered for another 30 minutes. Serve hot.

If You Are Freezing for Later
Allow the veggie bake to cool down completely. Cover with a layer of plastic wrap, then cover with an additional layer of aluminum foil.

When you're ready to cook, preheat the oven to 400°F. Remove the plastic wrap and aluminum foil and cook uncovered for 30 to 40 minutes until the veggie bake is completely hot all the way through.

tomato, feta, and corn grits

Grits are that perfect mix of creamy and hearty, and a bonus for anyone who is gluten-free or looking to avoid heavier grains. But I think the image of grits has been too wrapped up in the classic shrimp and grits, so hopefully this completely different take can change some minds. This 15-minute meal pulls together easily and also holds nicely in the freezer. You could use the same flavor profiles with another grain—farro, rice, or quinoa would also work well—but give the grits a chance and you might find that they become your new favorite go-to.

Serving: 8

Ingredients
7 cups liquid (any combination of broth, milk, or water)
2 cups stone-ground grits
1 teaspoon salt, plus more as needed
4 small tomatoes, diced
2 cups corn (previously frozen is fine if it is defrosted)
2 cups basil, chopped
1½ cups feta, crumbled

Put the liquid in a pot on medium-high heat and bring to a boil. Add the grits and salt, stir, lower the heat, and cover. Cook for 10 to 12 minutes, stirring every minute or two until the grits have come together.

If You Are Eating Now
Add the remaining ingredients and stir together for another 2 minutes. Serve hot.

If You Are Freezing for Later
Allow the grits to completely cool down, then add the remaining ingredients and fully combine. Split into single servings and freeze in freezer-safe containers or plastic bags. When you are ready to eat, reheat 1 minute at a time in a microwave. You may want to add a bit of water or milk to reconstitute if needed.

buttery lentils with spinach

This recipe is inspired by the great Punjabi delight, dal makhani. Its English translation is buttery lentils, and it is a silky, rich powerhouse of a dish. This recipe is a riff on that dish, but the cooking time is much shorter, and some greens are added to turn it into more of a one-pot meal. Instead of whole black lentils called urad dal or black gram, this recipe uses beluga lentils (which is what you find when you buy a bag labeled black lentils in most grocery stores). If you don't have garam masala, you can substitute with curry powder and a dash of cardamom, allspice, and/or clove. With the butter, sour cream, and spices, you'll still get the creamy texture that is reminiscent of the classic dish.

Serving: 8

Ingredients
4 cups black lentils

2 teaspoons salt, plus more as needed

12 tablespoons unsalted butter

⅔ cup (2 large or 4–6 small) grated shallots

2 tablespoons diced ginger

10 garlic cloves, diced

2 tablespoons garam masala

½ teaspoon turmeric

2 teaspoons cinnamon

2 tablespoons tomato puree

32 ounces chopped frozen spinach

1 cup sour cream

Bring 8 cups of water to a boil in a large pot and add the lentils and salt. Reduce the heat and let simmer, covered, for 30 minutes or until the lentils have fully cooked. Drain any remaining water from the lentils.

When the lentils are almost done, melt the butter in a saucepan. Add the shallots, ginger, garlic, garam masala, turmeric, cinnamon, and tomato puree. Cook for 5 minutes, stirring frequently. Add in the frozen spinach and cook until spinach is completely defrosted and incorporated into the sauce, up to 5 minutes. Add the lentils and sour cream to the mixture and combine fully. Add any additional salt to taste (don't be shy, this dish shines with the right amount of salt).

If You Are Eating Now
Cook an additional 5 minutes and serve hot.

If You Are Freezing for Later
Allow the lentils to completely cool. Place in freezer-safe containers or resealable freezer bags in single-serving portions. When ready to reheat, microwave for 1 minute at a time, stirring in between, until hot.

·········· portobello mushrooms ··········
with goat cheese

This recipe achieves that wonderful double bonus of being quick to make and quick to reheat. Portobellos are filling while also fulfilling any dietary restrictions; they cook quickly and add a meaty flavor without being obtrusive; and, lesser known, they hold up in the freezer like a dream. You can heat these up as a quick vegetarian side or have them as an entire meal. Either way, you'll have something delicious on the table in minutes.

Serving: 16

Ingredients
16 Portobello mushrooms, stems removed
Dash extra-virgin olive oil
Dash salt, plus more as needed
2 shallots, diced
1 cup (8-ounces) goat cheese at room
temperature
Juice of 2 lemons
2 cups roughly chopped spinach

Place the top rack in the oven 8 inches or so from the top. Turn the broiler on. Place the mushrooms on an aluminum foil-lined sheet pan. Coat the mushrooms on both sides with olive oil and salt and place the smooth side up on the pan and into the oven. Cook for 7 minutes.

Combine the shallots with the goat cheese and lemon juice, whisking well. Fold in the spinach and an additional dash of salt.

If You Are Eating Now
Remove the mushrooms from the oven, flip, and top with the goat cheese mixture. Cook another 4 minutes and serve hot.

If You Are Freezing for Later
Remove the mushrooms from the oven and allow them to cool completely. Flip them over and top with the goat cheese mixture. Wrap each in aluminum foil or plastic wrap and place them all in a freezer-safe container.

When you are ready to eat, remove the mushrooms from their wrapping and place on a plate in the microwave. Microwave for 1 minute at a time until hot and ready to eat.

eggplant parmesan

Some things are classic for a reason. Eggplant parm is the ultimate freezer food because it somehow holds up more perfectly than almost anything else no matter how much you deviate from the recipe or how long you leave it in the freezer. This might not look like the Italian American version you know, due to its lack of breading, but this is a take on what they serve in southern Italy. This dish is easier and healthier – with no frying involved - but keep in mind that the ingredients here truly matter. Buy a high-quality mozzarella and marinara sauce, and try to shy away from the huge eggplants because their seeds will add a lot of bitterness. You can slice them and salt them for a few hours, but I find that that's a step too far when medium-sized eggplants are just as readily available. The main thing to keep in mind is that this dish is meant to be easy.

Serving: 8

Ingredients
4 medium or 6 small eggplants
Heavy drizzle extra-virgin olive oil
Dash salt, plus more as needed
2 pounds mozzarella (Buffalo preferred)
32 ounces marinara sauce
1 cup basil
2 cups grated Parmesan cheese, plus more as needed

Make sure the top rack of your oven is approximately 4 inches from the top. Turn on your oven's broiler. Slice your eggplants crosswise into ½ inch discs. Place them on a sheet pan with a healthy drizzle of olive oil on both sides. Add a generous dash of salt and place them under the broiler for 4 minutes, or until the eggplants have softened. You will want to do this in batches so that the eggplants don't overlap. While the eggplant cooks, slice or dice the mozzarella as thin as you can.

In oven and freezer-safe dishes, build the eggplant parmesan. Start with a layer of marinara sauce on the bottom. Add a layer of eggplant. Add a thin layer of mozzarella, a dash of salt, then roughly tear some basil on top. Cover with a thin layer of the Parmesan, then start the same process again. Layer until you have almost reached the top of the dish, then sprinkle a heavier layer of Parmesan on top.

If You Are Eating Now
Preheat your oven to 350°F. Place the dish in the oven for 30 minutes. You can broil at the last minute if you would like a bit of browning on the cheese. Remove from the oven and allow to cool for a couple of minutes before serving.

If You Are Freezing for Later
Make sure all ingredients are cool (if you are not cooking now you will want to let the eggplant cool down as much as possible before touching the cheese). Cover the dish (or

(Continued on next page)

dishes) with a lid or plastic wrap and aluminum foil, being sure to get out as much air as possible. Place into the freezer.

When you are ready to eat, preheat the oven to 375°F. Remove the covering from the dish and place into the oven. For 2 servings, cook for at least 40 minutes and increase the timing from there, depending on how large the dish is. A good rule of thumb is to add another 10 minutes or so for every serving. If you're doing more than 4 servings, you can cover the dish for the first hour as needed. You can broil at the last minute if you would like a bit of browning on the cheese. Remove from the oven and allow to cool for a couple of minutes before serving.

cauliflower mac and cheese

Cauliflower "mac and cheese" is a dish that has become ubiquitous as people try to cut carbs, but I've always found it a bit lacking, so this recipe has a few tricks up its sleeve. By roasting the cauliflower, you can keep a better texture, especially when freezing. By adding quinoa, you keep some substance in there without the macaroni. Last, a little bit of turmeric not only adds depth to the flavor, but also adds color. What you get is a vibrant, cheesy dish that'll make you forget the macaroni in mac and cheese.

Serving: 6–8

Ingredients
3 pounds cauliflower
3 tablespoons olive oil
2 teaspoons kosher salt, divided
1 cup quinoa
1½ cups whole milk
8 ounces cream cheese
½ teaspoon turmeric
1 teaspoon Dijon mustard
2 cups sharp cheddar cheese, shredded
Juice of ½ lemon

Preheat oven to 450°F. Cut cauliflower into florets. Toss with the olive oil and ½ teaspoon salt, then place on a sheet pan. Cook in the oven for approximately 13 to 15 minutes until they are tender enough to eat but still crisp. Set aside to cool down.

Bring 1 cup of water to a boil in a saucepan. Add the quinoa and ½ teaspoon salt, then reduce heat to a simmer. Cook for 12 to 15 minutes or until the water has fully absorbed. Set aside, uncovered, to cool down.

Meanwhile, place a saucepan on medium heat. Add the milk, cream cheese, turmeric, mustard, cheddar cheese, and remaining salt. Stir constantly until smooth, making sure to never let it reach a boil, about 3 to 4 minutes. Allow the cheese mixture to cool down.

When all your parts are cooled down to room temperature, combine and add lemon juice.

If You Are Eating Now
Turn down the oven to 350°F. Add the mixture to a casserole dish and cover with aluminum foil. Cook for 20 to 40 minutes, depending on the size of the dish and how deep it is. You'll know it is done when the top starts to bubble. Remove the foil and turn on the broiler for 2 to 4 minutes to brown the top. Serve hot.

If You Are Freezing for Later
Place the mixture into casserole dishes (be careful to spread them out so you can heat smaller portion sizes later). Cover with an airtight lid or a layer of plastic wrap and aluminum foil.

(Continued on next page)

To cook, preheat the oven to 350°F. Remove the lid and cover with foil. Bake for 30 to 45 minutes, depending on the size of your dish. Remove the cover and bake an additional 10 to 15 minutes, until the mac and cheese is just barely bubbling. Turn the broiler on for 2 to 4 minutes to brown the top. Serve hot.

If you have frozen individual portions, you can microwave this dish as well (but only with small portions, otherwise it will overcook). Cook in 1-minute intervals, stirring in between, until it is hot.

red pepper quiche

Few things hold up better in the freezer than a quiche. Pop it back in the oven after a few weeks or months frozen and you won't even be able to tell the difference. Because peppers are made up of over 90 percent water, their moisture will keep this quiche as fluffy and moist as if it were brand new. The top might "weep" a bit, but that's totally normal. You can either blot it or just leave it. What you'll be left with is a flavorful, healthy dish that makes for a perfect breakfast or dinner without doing anything more than turning on your oven.

Serving: 6–8

Ingredients
1 pie crust (recipe on page 244)
2 red or yellow peppers, cut into 1-inch slices
2 tablespoons chopped chives
½ cup milk
5 eggs, beaten
2 teaspoons garlic powder
2 teaspoons salt

Preheat the oven to 350°F. Place the crust in a pie pan and crimp the edges to your liking. In a bowl, combine the peppers, chives, milk, eggs, garlic powder, and salt. Pour the mixture into the pie crust. Bake for 40 to 50 minutes or until the quiche has just set.

If You Are Eating Now
Cool for at least 5 minutes before serving. You can serve hot or cold.

If You Are Freezing for Later
Let the quiche come completely to room temperature. Wrap tightly in heavy-duty plastic wrap and place in the freezer. When you are ready to eat, preheat the oven to 350°F. Bake for 50 minutes to 1 hour, or until the quiche is fully reheated all the way through. Remove from the oven and serve hot.

single-serving lasagna

This recipe takes one of the great freezer classics and gives it a new spin. Ricotta and anchovies (trust me, you won't even know they are there!) give the dish richness and depth without as much prep time. Beyond the flavor, this version gives you something that most freezer lasagnas won't: portion control. By putting individual lasagnas into muffin tins, you eliminate the worst parts of freezer lasagna. They cook faster and if you're only hankering for one piece, you don't have to reheat an entire large lasagna.

Serving: 24

Ingredients

1 medium yellow onion, minced

Drizzle extra-virgin olive oil

1 teaspoon dried oregano

1 teaspoon dried basil

4 garlic cloves, minced

2 pounds lean ground beef

2 ounces anchovies, chopped

1½ teaspoons salt, plus more as needed

¼ teaspoon ground black pepper

3 cups (24 ounces) plain marinara sauce

24 lasagna noodles

2 cups (16 ounces) ricotta cheese

1 egg, beaten

1 cup thinly diced mozzarella cheese

½ cup chopped basil leaves

2 cups grated Parmesan cheese, plus more to sprinkle on top

Optional:

Foil baking cups

In a large saucepan on medium-high heat, cook the onion with olive oil for 5 to 7 minutes until the onions start to look translucent and have browned a bit. Add the oregano, basil, garlic, beef, anchovies, salt, and pepper and cook another 5 to 7 minutes, without stirring too much, until the meat browns a bit. Add the marinara sauce and let the mixture simmer, covered, for 30 minutes, stirring occasionally.

While the sauce is cooking, bring a pot of salted water to a boil. Cook the lasagna noodles for 8 to 10 minutes until they are just cooked through but still al dente. Drain the noodles and rinse them under cold water. Find a water or wine glass that is roughly the size of a single cup in the muffin tin. Using the top of the glass, cut circles out of the pasta to create the layers that will make up the lasagna. You can usually get 3 full circles and 2 half circles out of each noodle. Twenty-four lasagna noodles should make enough full circles, but it is good to have the half ones as well, in case some of the circles rip. (Note: Because you are cutting circles from the pasta, you will definitely have leftover pasta. Keep this in mind and make a pasta salad out of it or something else.) Set to the side. Combine the ricotta, egg, mozzarella cheese, and basil in a bowl.

(Continued on next page)

To assemble, grease each muffin tin. If you are freezing, you can choose to line with aluminum foil or foil baking cups. Add a bottom layer of noodle, a very thin layer of the ricotta mixture on top, and another layer of noodle. Then, add a layer of meat, a layer of the ricotta mixture, a bit of Parmesan cheese, then another noodle. Do this until they reach the top, ending with a noodle layer. You want to make sure that the noodles on top are curling down, not up. Then, sprinkle some more Parmesan cheese on top.

If You Are Eating Now

Preheat oven to 375°F. Cook for 35 to 40 minutes. Cool for 15 minutes before serving.

If You Are Freezing for Later

If you are freezing, make sure to assemble with aluminum foil or foil baking cups so that you can remove the lasagnas once they are frozen—you don't want to make all of these individualized portions only to find that you can't get them out of a full 12-count muffin tin. You can also buy the disposable aluminum muffin tins and cut the tins apart with scissors in whatever portion size you want whenever you are ready to cook.

Once you have your lasagnas assembled, place them in the freezer. If you want to leave them in the tin, cover with plastic wrap, then aluminum foil tightly and place in the freezer. If you want to make room in your freezer, after a few hours you can remove the frozen lasagnas from the muffin tin and place them in a freezer-safe bag.

To cook, preheat the oven to 375°F. Place however many lasagnas you are heating up into a muffin tin. Cover with foil and bake for 40 to 45 minutes. Remove the foil and cook another 10 minutes until the top is golden and the lasagna is cooked all the way through.

pea fusilli with bacon

Pasta is often viewed as a heavy meal, but this bright pea dish will change the narrative. This recipe freezes well because the sauce is light and almost like a pesto, so it doesn't add a lot of water to the proceedings, and the textured pasta cooked a little bit al dente holds up well once it has been cooked. The added unctuous flavor of bacon packs an extra punch. Simply reheat this pasta or let it defrost and serve at room temperature for an outdoor, summery meal.

Serving: 8–10

Ingredients
1 pound bacon, finely chopped
1 large yellow onion, diced
3 garlic cloves, minced
6 cups frozen peas, divided
2 cups chopped basil, divided
Juice of 1 lemon
2 pounds (32 ounces) fusilli pasta
1 teaspoon salt, plus more as needed

Bring a pot of salted water to a boil. Place a separate pot on medium-high heat and add the bacon. Cook for 5 to 7 minutes or until the bacon is to your preferred level of doneness. Remove the bacon but not the bacon drippings. Add the onion and garlic and cook for another 5 to 7 minutes until the onions are translucent and begin to brown. Add in 3 cups frozen peas and 1 cup basil and cook another 2 to 3 minutes until the peas have softened. Add in the lemon juice and blend in a blender or with an immersion blender. If the sauce isn't blending enough or feels too thick, you can add in up to 2 cups of water as needed (it should still feel thick like a pesto, but thin enough to be a sauce on a pasta). Add salt to the sauce as needed.

While the bacon is cooking, add pasta to the pot of salted water. Cook for approximately 9 minutes or a few minutes shy of the cooking time on the packaging, ensuring that it remains very al dente, or just barely cooked enough to eat. (If you are freezing the pasta you really want to give it a lot of leeway.) Drain the water and set the pasta aside.

If You Are Eating Now
Add the bacon and the rest of the peas and basil to the sauce and cook for an additional 2 minutes, or until the peas have just softened and the sauce is hot. Combine the pasta with the sauce. Serve hot.

If You Are Freezing for Later
Let the pasta and sauce cool down, then add the bacon along with the rest of the peas and basil to the sauce. Fully combine the pasta and sauce together, then place in freezer-safe containers. Make sure to divide the pasta into

single portions and as flat as possible as you freeze to ensure that the pasta doesn't overcook when reheated.

When you are ready to reheat, you can allow the pasta to defrost in the fridge or cook it straight from frozen. Put the pasta in a microwave-safe container and heat 1 minute at a time, turning and/or stirring as you go. Timing will depend on the size of the portion.

pork and chive orzo

One of my favorite food cities is Taipei, Taiwan. Everywhere you turn is another food market or cluster of restaurants where tradition and innovation seem to collide seamlessly, but one of Taipei's dishes that most knocked my socks off was also the simplest: a bowl of minced pork with Chinese chives over rice. My version is reminiscent of the original while using readily available ingredients to create a dish that is comforting and hearty without being heavy. And by using orzo instead of rice it freezes like a dream. This is the recipe I make for picnics and birthday parties when I need a dish that can work at any temperature. It is different yet a total crowd pleaser.

Serving: 8

Ingredients

1 pound orzo
2 tablespoons vegetable or canola oil
6 cups (15 ounces) chopped scallions
5 garlic cloves, minced
3 pounds ground pork
4 tablespoons soy sauce, divided
2 tablespoons sesame oil, divided
1 teaspoon grated ginger
1/8 teaspoon chili powder
1 teaspoon salt
Juice of 1/2 lemon
1 (15-ounce) can black beans, drained

Bring a pot of salted water to a boil and put a large wide-brimmed pan, like a Dutch oven, on very high heat. Add the orzo to the pot and the oil to the pan. Add the scallions and garlic to the pan and cook for 3 minutes, stirring occasionally. You should see them start to get very soft and brown. Add in the pork along with 2 tablespoons soy sauce, 1 tablespoon sesame oil, ginger, chili powder, and salt. Break up the meat and allow it to brown. When the orzo has cooked for approximately 7 minutes (you want it to be cooked but still al dente), drain it in a colander. Turn the heat off the pan with the pork and add in the orzo, lemon juice, black beans, and remaining soy sauce and sesame oil. Stir to combine and serve.

If You Are Freezing for Later

For whatever portion you are freezing, allow it to cool completely to room temperature, then place in single-serving freezer containers and remove as much air as possible. When you are ready to eat the orzo, remove and microwave, 1 minute at a time, until it is hot. If you are unfreezing a large batch you can add a touch of water to bring back the consistency. You can also add a bit more soy sauce or chili powder if it needs more flavor after freezing.

zucchini marinara with rigatoni

This version of classic marinara takes the tomato sauce we know and love and gives it a bit of a vegetable flair. It's also a great recipe for kids, since the vegetables are hidden a bit.

Serving: 8–10

Ingredients

6 cups (2 pounds) chopped tomatoes
6 garlic cloves, chopped
1 tablespoon chopped basil
1 teaspoon salt, plus more as needed
Dash pepper
2 medium zucchinis, halved lengthwise
1 small yellow onion, roughly diced
Extra-virgin olive oil for brushing
2 pounds rigatoni

Turn on your oven's broiler and bring a pot of salted water to a boil. Place the tomatoes, garlic, basil, salt, and pepper in a separate saucepan on high heat. Cook for 5 minutes, stirring occasionally, or until the tomatoes have started to break down and become a liquid that has started to boil. Turn the heat to medium high (so it is still at a low boil) and allow to cook for 10 to 15 more minutes, stirring occasionally, until the sauce has started to form and has the texture of a typical tomato sauce. While the sauce is cooking, place the zucchinis and onion on a sheet pan and brush them with olive oil. Place the pan under the broiler for 5 to 8 minutes, or until the zucchinis and onion have cooked and are heavily browned and just starting to char. Add the pasta to the boiling water and cook according to package instructions. Take the pasta out and drain it when it is edible but al dente. Add the zucchinis and onion to the tomato sauce and blend in a blender or with a hand blender. Add salt to taste. I like to keep the sauce fairly chunky, but the texture is up to you.

If You Are Eating Now

Combine the sauce with the pasta and serve hot.

If You Are Freezing for Later

Allow the sauce and pasta to come down to room temperature separately. Combine, then place in individual servings in freezer-safe containers or resealable bags. Place in the freezer. When you are ready to eat, you can either defrost the pasta or cook straight from frozen. Put the pasta in a microwave-safe container and heat 1 minute at a time, turning and/or stirring as you go.

········· the southern-italian ·········
mashup spaghetti bake

I grew up in South Carolina but my obsession with Italy is well documented, so I really couldn't love anything more than a mashup of my two favorite places, and this recipe brings a bit of the best from both worlds (and, yes, I know Southern Italian usually conjures thoughts of Sicily). Spaghetti and tomato are classic Italian. But collards and casseroles are all about the south. And the bacon, well, let's call that the major overlap from both cultures. Unlike a lot of casserole recipes, this one feels lighter because of the heavy presence of greens, but the thick texture of collards belongs in such a warming, homey dish. Not to mention that it holds up great in the freezer. Take the best of two wonderful worlds and keep this recipe on hand.

Serving: 6–8

Ingredients

1 pound (16 ounces) dry spaghetti
½ pound bacon, diced
1 large yellow onion, diced
6 cups (2 bunches) roughly chopped collard greens
6 garlic cloves, chopped
Extra-virgin olive oil as needed
1 (28-ounce) can chopped tomatoes
Dash salt
½ cup grated Parmesan cheese

Place a large heavy skillet or Dutch oven on medium-high heat and bring a pot of salted water to boil. Add the spaghetti to the water and cook for 7 to 10 minutes. Remove it from heat and drain when it is almost done cooking but al dente. Set aside to cool.

While the spaghetti is cooking, add the bacon to the skillet and cook for 5 to 7 minutes (the bacon should still be very uncooked), then add the onion. Cook for another 5 to 7 minutes, until the onion starts to soften, then add the collards and garlic. Cook for 10 to 12 minutes, or until the collards are fully soft. Add olive oil as needed, stirring frequently. When the collards are ready, add the tomatoes and salt. Add the pasta to the sauce and mix.

If You Are Eating Now

Preheat the oven to 375°F. Place the mixture in smaller casserole containers or a large skillet. Sprinkle the Parmesan cheese on top. Put the casserole in the oven for 15 to 20 minutes. Serve hot.

If You Are Freezing for Later

Let the pasta completely cool, then place in freezer-safe dishes that are also ovenproof. Sprinkle the Parmesan cheese on top. Place a layer of plastic wrap on top, then cover it completely. Place the container in the freezer. When you are ready to eat, preheat the oven to 375°F. Put the casserole in the oven for 30 to 40 minutes. Cook time will depend on your portion size. Serve hot.

teriyaki carbonara

Sometimes inspiration comes from the most unexpected of places. When I was in Boise, Idaho, our friends mentioned their favorite place to get takeout had a dish that combined teriyaki sauce and carbonara. I was both curious and dubious, but when the dish came, I was in love! Why wouldn't creamy dairy meld well with the tang of teriyaki sauce? I knew I had to make my own version.

Serving: 8

Ingredients
4 pounds chicken breast
1½ cups teriyaki sauce, divided
Dash salt
2 pounds spaghetti
1 cup heavy cream
4 eggs
2 cups grated Parmesan cheese
8 scallions, chopped

Bring a pot of salted water to a boil and turn the oven on broil, making sure the top rack is approximately 4 inches from the top.

Cut up the chicken breast into bite-sized pieces. Toss the chicken in a bowl with ½ cup teriyaki sauce. Place aluminum foil on a sheet pan and spread the chicken on top. Sprinkle salt.

Put the spaghetti in the boiling water and put the chicken under the broiler. While the pasta and chicken are cooking, combine the cream, eggs, cheese, and scallions into a pot with the remaining teriyaki sauce. Whisk and turn the heat on low.

If You Are Eating Now
Cook both the pasta and the chicken for approximately 7 to 9 minutes, or until the chicken is almost fully cooked and the pasta is edible but al dente. Combine the chicken and spaghetti in the pot with the sauce and cook for another minute until it has come together. Serve hot.

If You Are Freezing for Later
Cook the pasta and chicken for 6 to 7 minutes, or until the chicken is almost cooked and the pasta is very al dente but still edible. Drain the pasta. Remove the pot with the creamy teriyaki mixture from the heat and add the chicken and spaghetti. Combine fully and allow the pasta to completely cool down. Divide the pasta into individual servings in resealable freezer-safe bags or containers, removing as much air as possible. Place in the freezer. Even if you plan to eat this dish with another person, it is important to freeze each portion separately or the pasta will overcook when it reheats.

When you are ready to eat, heat the pasta in the microwave in a microwave-safe bowl for 1 minute at a time, stirring in between, until hot.

spicy salami-pesto pasta

Pasta that goes in the freezer needs a sauce that hits with a bang. This is one of those sauces that has a lot going on but somehow melds together so that every strong flavor combines to be greater than the individual parts. This pasta is great fresh from the pot, microwaved back to life, or even defrosted and served cold. Who knew salami from a blender could be so great?

Serving: 8–10

Ingredients
2 cups basil
½ pound thinly sliced salami
4 large garlic cloves
½ cup grated pecorino
1 cup sunflower seeds
2 cups extra-virgin olive oil
2 pounds rigatoni
Salt to taste

In a blender, combine the basil, salami, garlic, pecorino, sunflower seeds, and olive oil. Bring a salted pot of water to boil. Add the rigatoni and cook for 7 to 9 minutes. You want the pasta to be cooked but still al dente—*very* al dente if you are freezing. Drain the pasta.

If You Are Eating Now
Add the rigatoni to the salami pesto and combine. Taste to see if any additional salt is needed. Serve hot.

If You Are Freezing for Later
Let the pasta fully cool down (as quickly as possible so it doesn't continue cooking), then combine with the pesto. Taste to see if any additional salt is needed. Place in a freezer-safe container or resealable bag. If you want to eat the pasta straight from frozen, it reheats much more easily if it is individually portioned and flat.

Defrost or heat directly from frozen in the microwave. You can add a bit of olive oil or water to reconstitute but be careful to add slowly. Stir frequently as you heat to make sure you don't overdo it.

parmesan butter linguine

Sometimes the simplest recipes are the ones we end up obsessing over the most. I served this to my family for dinner one night and my sister looked at it and commented, "Is this it?" But somehow the whole pot was gone within a few minutes. You can't really go wrong with the trifecta of butter, Parmesan, and lemon. The hints of garlic and tarragon bring it all together. And because of its simplicity and comforting flavor profile, this recipe makes for one of the best items to have in the freezer. Just make sure to get good ingredients. Real Parmesan cheese, a high-quality butter, and fresh lemon juice will all stand out.

Serving: 8

Ingredients

2 pounds dry linguine

16 tablespoons unsalted butter

¼ cup chopped tarragon (or more to your taste)

4 garlic cloves, minced

Juice of 2 lemons

1 teaspoon salt

2 cups grated Parmesan cheese

Bring a pot of salted water to a boil. Add the linguine and cook for 8 to 10 minutes. You want the pasta to be edible but still al dente—if you are freezing you want to make sure it is even more al dente. Drain and set aside when done.

While the pasta is cooking, start making the butter mixture. In a large skillet on medium heat, melt the butter. Once it has completely melted, let it cook for about 2 minutes, stirring occasionally, until it begins to brown a bit. Add the tarragon and garlic. Continue to stir until the butter has browned completely, approximately another 4 to 6 minutes. It should have a nutty smell but not be close to burning (if your butter does burn you unfortunately need to start over).

Turn the heat off and allow the butter to cool for a few minutes. Combine the lemon juice, salt, and drained pasta with the butter. Once it is completely coated, stir in the Parmesan. Make sure to mix in that order, otherwise the cheese will clump. If eating now, serve hot.

If You Are Freezing for Later

Allow the pasta to completely cool, then place it in individual portions in a freezer-safe container or bag. Because this is a thinner pasta you really don't want to overheat it, so individual portions are crucial. Remove as much air as possible from your containers or bags.

When you are ready to eat again, put the pasta in the microwave (in a microwave-safe container or bowl) and heat 1 minute at a time until hot.

gorgonzola radicchio pasta

I once went on a tour of a pasta factory in Italy where the owner said one of their most popular flavor combinations was gorgonzola and radicchio because the bitterness of the radicchio melds perfectly with the tangy softness of the gorgonzola. When I tried this combo at home, I was hooked. This is the ultimate dish because it takes literally the same amount of time as it takes to boil pasta. The key here if you are freezing is to really undercook the orecchiette because it keeps cooking as it cools down (since it is still hot). This is a pasta to make a batch of, then keep half in your freezer for a busy day.

Serving: 8

Ingredients
2 pounds orecchiette (or another small pasta)
3 large heads radicchio
2 cups chopped or slivered almonds
16 ounces crumbled gorgonzola
Dash salt

Bring a salted pot of water to a boil and turn on your oven's broiler, making sure that one rack is very close to the top. Place the pasta in the water and cook for approximately 7 to 10 minutes, making sure it is very al dente. While the pasta is cooking, chop the radicchio very roughly—each leaf should be in approximately 3 pieces, so that they are still sizable. Place on a greased sheet pan and put directly under the broiler for 1 minute, or until the radicchio has started to brown. Remove and set aside.

When the pasta is al dente (especially al dente if you are freezing) but ready to eat, drain, then place it back in the pot. Add in the radicchio, almonds, gorgonzola, and salt. Stir until the cheese has melted slightly. If you are eating now, serve hot.

If You Are Freezing for Later
Allow the pasta to completely cool (spreading it out, if you can, on the sheet pan so it cools faster and doesn't overcook the pasta), then place in freezer-safe containers or bags. Make sure to portion it out if you want to keep individual portions and remove as much air as possible. Try not to freeze in too large a chunk or it will overcook in reheating.

When you are ready to eat again, you can either defrost the pasta overnight in the fridge or cook it straight from frozen. Put the pasta in the microwave (in a microwave-safe container) and heat 1 minute at a time until hot.

ricotta gnocchi

These ricotta gnocchi are the lighter and easier cousin to the more famous potato gnocchi, yet somehow, they take the same amount of time as boxed pasta. And that isn't even the best part: these actually get better once they freeze. These gnocchi are always light as air, but when they cook from frozen, they also manage to have a cheesier interior that takes the whole dish to the next level.

Serving: 8

Ingredients
5 cups (32 ounces) firm whole-milk ricotta
2 cups freshly grated Parmesan cheese
1 teaspoon salt
4 egg yolks
1 cup all-purpose flour, plus more for dusting
Butter or other pasta sauce (to your taste)

Make sure your ricotta is not too wet. If it is, you can drain it over paper towels on top of a colander or use a cheese cloth and weigh it down. Once your ricotta is ready, combine it with the Parmesan, salt, and egg yolks. Add in the flour and combine gently. If the dough feels too wet to roll out (either from your ricotta or if you had particularly large egg yolks), add a bit more flour into the dough.

Add a bit of flour to your surface. Taking the dough into pieces, roll out each piece into a long cylinder, approximately the width and shape of a breadstick, or about ½ inch. While you will need to roll the dough a fair amount, try to knead it as little as possible, and sprinkling with flour a bit as needed. Cut the dough into 1-inch pieces and set aside.

If You Are Eating Now
Bring a pot of water to a boil. Add the gnocchi into the water (don't let the raw gnocchi sit out too long or they will get dry) and let them cook for approximately 2 minutes, or until the gnocchi start to float. Remove the gnocchi from the pot with a slotted spoon and immediately combine with butter or sauce.

If You Are Freezing for Later
To freeze the gnocchi, place them on a parchment-lined pan, ensuring that they are not touching, and place them in the freezer. Once they have fully frozen (1 to 2 hours) move them into a resealable freezer-safe bag, making sure to remove as much air as possible.

When you are ready to eat them, bring a pot of water to a boil. Add the gnocchi into the water and let them cook for 2 to 3 minutes, or until the gnocchi start to float. Remove the gnocchi from the pot with a slotted spoon and immediately combine with butter or sauce.

chapter 6

meats

goat cheese and
olive-stuffed chicken

When I first met my now-husband, I wanted to cook him dinner, but I was nervous about making the right thing. He had already told me about his mother's incredible skills in the kitchen so I wanted to make something impressive, but on a college student's budget I couldn't break the bank, so I came up with this recipe. It has become a staple ever since—my sister-in-law now eats goat cheese because of it. It is different without having difficult ingredients, and is also great in the freezer because brining the chicken keeps it moist no matter what. Make this recipe to impress someone without a lot of effort.

Serving: 6–8

Ingredients
¼ cup salt, plus more as needed
6 pounds large boneless skinless chicken breasts
2 garlic cloves
2 cups goat cheese
⅔ cup finely chopped olives
1 tablespoon herbes de Provence
Juice of 1 lemon, divided
1 tablespoon extra-virgin olive oil

Brine the chicken breasts: Combine the salt in a pot with 2 cups hot water and stir until it fully dissolves. Add 6 cups cold water and stir together, making sure your water is now at least room temperature (you don't want to cook your chicken yet). Add in the chicken and place the pot in the fridge. You want to keep it in the fridge for up to 1 hour (you can do as little as 15 minutes if you are short on time, but just try not to go over 1 hour).

Next, make the goat cheese dressing: Using a Microplane or very thin grater, grate the garlic cloves into a bowl. Add the goat cheese, olives, herbes de Provence, and ½ lemon juice. Mix very well. Remove your chicken and pat it down so that it is no longer wet. Salt it on both sides.

Then, make the pockets for the goat cheese: Take a sharp knife and cut lengthwise in the center of the chicken, leaving about ½ inch at the top and bottom, and ensuring that you do not cut all the way through. Inside the chicken, cut horizontally to expand the pocket. Essentially, you are cutting a small pouch within the chicken to stuff, and you want to be sure not to cut through any side or the goat

(Continued on next page)

cheese mixture will not stay inside, so work carefully. When you have cut your chicken pockets, add the goat cheese mixture inside, stuffing it so that the mixture is even throughout. Place a pan on medium-high heat and add the remaining lemon juice and olive oil. Once the pan is hot, add the chicken cut-side down on the pan and brown for 4 to 5 minutes. Turn it over and brown for 2 additional minutes.

If You Are Eating Now

Preheat your oven to 350°F. Place the pan with the chicken in the oven, or place the chicken on a lined sheet pan, for 30 to 45 minutes, depending on size. You can always cut into it a bit to see if it is done or use a meat thermometer. The internal temperature should be 155°F when you remove it from the oven (so it will rise to 165°F once rested). Serve hot.

If You Are Freezing for Later

Remove the chicken from the pan and allow it to cool completely to room temperature. Wrap each piece of chicken tightly in a layer of either plastic wrap or parchment paper, then wrap it again in aluminum foil. Place all the chicken breasts in a freezer-safe resealable bag or container in the freezer. When you are ready to cook, you can make the chicken either from defrosted or straight from frozen, depending on your preference. The chicken will be slightly more moist if you allow it time to defrost, but either method will work.

To heat from defrosted: Remove the chicken from the freezer and place in the refrigerator for 12 to 24 hours before cooking. Preheat the oven to 350°F. Remove the chicken from its packaging and place it on a lined sheet pan. Place it in the oven for 35 to 45 minutes, depending on the size of the chicken. The internal temperature should be 155°F when you remove it from the oven (so it will rise to 165°F once rested). Serve hot.

To heat from frozen: Preheat the oven to 350°F. Remove the chicken from its packaging and place it on a lined sheet pan. Place in the oven for approximately 1 hour, depending on the size of the chicken. The internal temperature should be 160°F when you remove it from the oven (so it will rise to 165°F once rested). Serve hot.

sausage gomae

One of my favorite Japanese side dishes is Gomae, a vegetable (usually spinach when you see it in an American restaurant) cooked with sesame dressing. It is the perfect cross between a salad and a side dish, with bold flavors encouraging you to eat your vegetables. I find the sesame dressing addictive, and you could replace the sausage with almost any meat and still have a winner. I also love the use of already frozen spinach here because it saves you from the typical spinach issue of turning a giant amount into a teeny tiny portion once it is cooked. This 15-minute meal can also hold up to freezing when needed.

Serving: 8

Ingredients
2 pounds pork sausage
¼ cup rice vinegar, divided
¼ cup tahini
¼ cup soy sauce
¼ cup sesame oil
4 pounds frozen spinach, defrosted
1 cup sesame seeds
Dash salt

Put a large pan or Dutch oven on medium-high heat. Cut the sausage into bite-sized pieces and add to the pan, flipping occasionally. In a separate bowl, combine 2 tablespoons rice vinegar, the tahini, soy sauce, and sesame oil. Set aside.

After the sausage has cooked for 5 minutes, add the remaining rice vinegar to the pan to deglaze. Add the spinach to the pan and cover for 1 to 2 minutes, or until it has heated up, then add the sesame dressing and toss everything together. Add the sesame seeds and a dash of salt and combine.

If You Are Freezing for Later
Allow the mixture to fully cool down, then place in individual servings in freezer-safe containers or bags. Put in the freezer. When you are ready to eat, heat in the microwave, 1 or 2 minutes at a time, stirring in between until hot.

sesame allspice chicken thighs

Chicken thighs are the best possible meat for facing the elements, and this recipe doubles down on making it great. Chicken thighs already start with a ton of flavor and tenderness but keeping in the bone helps retain that moisture as well. On top of that, you've got a thick skin that holds up, along with a marinade to add another layer of moisture. The combination of tahini and allspice might sound like a lot of flavor, but because it's a marinade and a lot cooks off, it's actually a very subtle combination, so make a batch for today, then throw a few in the freezer. You'll be ready when you need something to just throw in the oven.

Serving: 6–8

Ingredients
4 tablespoons tahini
1 tablespoon extra-virgin olive oil
2 teaspoons allspice
1 tablespoon salt
12 bone-in chicken thighs, skin on
Canola oil for cooking

Combine the tahini, olive oil, allspice, and salt in a large bowl. Add the chicken to the bowl and coat well. Marinate in the fridge for approximately 8 hours (you can go anywhere from 2 hours to overnight as needed).

Put a large cast-iron or heavy skillet over medium-high heat and add canola oil. Put the chicken in the skillet, skin-side down, and cook for 10 to 12 minutes, until the skin is golden brown. Shake the pan occasionally to stop the skin from sticking to the bottom and rotate the pan to evenly distribute the heat.

If You Are Eating Now
Preheat oven to 450°F. Move the skillet into the oven and cook for 8 to 10 more minutes so that the skin is crispy. Flip the chicken over and cook for 5 to 7 more minutes or until the chicken is cooked through, approximately 155°F. Let rest for at least 5 minutes before serving.

If You Are Freezing for Later
Remove the chicken thighs from the pan and let them cool completely. Wrap each thigh in plastic wrap tightly, then place all of them in a resealable freezer bag or container. Place in the freezer.

When you are ready to eat, heat the oven to 400°F. Remove the thighs from the plastic wrap and place on a sheet pan. Put them in the oven for 30 minutes or until they are cooked through, approximately 155°F. Remove from the oven and serve hot.

pomegranate chicken

I use pomegranates in everything sweet from smoothies to desserts, but it is also a particularly good partner for meat. It can cut through richness and bring out flavors that are otherwise hidden. This recipe aims to add as much power as possible to a dish coming out of your freezer. We start with bone-in chicken because it adds flavor while also helping to keep it moist. This recipe calls for pomegranate molasses, but don't worry if it's not an ingredient you can find in your local grocery store. To make it yourself, just pour 1½ cups pomegranate juice into a saucepan and bring it to a boil. Reduce the heat, add a touch of fresh lime juice and salt, then allow it to simmer until reduced into a molasses consistency (anywhere from 30 minutes to 1 hour, depending on the pan size). Once you start making it, you might just end up putting it on everything.

Serving: 10–12

Ingredients
1 tablespoon salt
¼ cup pomegranate molasses
1 tablespoon red wine vinegar
4 garlic cloves, finely chopped
2 whole (3–4 pound) chickens, divided into pieces
½ cup chicken stock
¼ cup (2–3) chopped shallots
1 cup chopped fresh parsley
1 cup fresh or dried pomegranate seeds

Combine the salt, pomegranate molasses, vinegar, and garlic in a bowl. Rub the chicken with the sauce, then place it in a large plastic resealable bag (you may want to use two). Shake the chicken to make sure it is evenly coated, then place it in the fridge. Keep it there to marinate for at least 1 hour, up to 6 hours.

When your chicken is ready, remove it from the fridge and preheat a large skillet (preferably cast iron if you have it) on high heat. Add the chicken stock and shallots and cook for 5 minutes or until the shallots have started to soften. Remove half of the chicken stock/shallots mixture (since you will have to coat the chicken in two batches) and add half of the chicken pieces, skin-side down. Let the chicken brown (don't move it too much) for 4 to 5 minutes. Remove the smaller items like the wings and the legs, then turn over the other pieces to cook for another 3 to 5 minutes (depending on the size of your pieces). Remove and repeat with the rest of the chicken, adding back in the rest of the chicken stock/shallots mixture.

If You Are Eating Now

Preheat the oven to 400°F. Add all the chicken back into the large skillet (or if you feel like you don't have enough room and you're eating everything now you can always use a large, lined sheet pan). Cover and bake for 30 minutes. Remove the cover and the smaller pieces of the chicken and cook another 15 minutes. Add the rest of the pieces back in, top with the parsley and pomegranate seeds, and cook for 5 to 10 minutes until the chicken is cooked to your desired doneness (or an internal temperature of 160°F).

If You Are Freezing for Later

Remove the chicken from the skillet and allow it to cool down fully. Take each piece of chicken and tightly wrap it individually in plastic wrap. Place all the chicken in a resealable freezer bag or container and freeze. You can choose to freeze the parsley and pomegranate seeds in a separate bag, or you can use them fresh whenever you want to make the chicken. When it is time to cook, you can either defrost the chicken or make it from frozen. If you have time to defrost, it makes for a slightly moister chicken, but either method works.

If defrosting, allow the chicken to defrost in the fridge for 12 to 24 hours. When you are ready to cook, preheat the oven to 400°F. Remove the chicken from its packaging, then place the chicken in a Dutch oven (or on a lined sheet pan if you don't have one) and cook, covered for 30 minutes. Remove the cover and the smaller chicken parts and cook for another 15 minutes. Add back in the rest of the pieces, top with the parsley and pomegranate, and cook for 5 to 10 minutes until the chicken is cooked to your desired doneness (or an internal temperature of 155°F).

If you are cooking straight from frozen, preheat the oven to 400°F. Remove the frozen chicken from its packaging and place it in a Dutch oven (or on a lined sheet pan if you don't have one) and cook, covered, for 50 minutes. Remove the cover and the smaller chicken parts and cook for another 15 minutes. Add back in the rest of the pieces, top with the parsley and pomegranate, and cook for 5 to 15 minutes until the chicken is cooked to your desired doneness (or an internal temperature of 155°F).

HAMburger

Sometimes I get a little giddy from a silly idea that actually works. The HAMburger was one of those ideas. I ran it by my brother over the phone and I kept saying the word as though it was brilliant. "Yeah, it's going to be a burger but with actual ham! A HAM-burger!" Of course, just because the pun was funny didn't mean that the actual recipe would be good, but once I made it, I was surprised we didn't do this more. For a culture obsessed with ground meat between a bun, why are we so stuck on beef? The secret to this burger is in doubling up on the pork and adding soy and Worcestershire sauces for some extra oomph. So, now you can have a delicious recipe and a silly pun.

Serving: 4–6

Ingredients

3 ounces bacon, chopped into small pieces

3 pounds ground pork

1 tablespoon salt

2 teaspoons soy sauce

2 teaspoons Worcestershire sauce

¼ cup vegetable oil, plus more as needed

Hamburger buns and condiments as needed

In a pan on medium-high heat, cook the bacon for 5 to 7 minutes. It is done when it is cooked enough to eat but not yet crispy. Set it aside to cool. Add the bacon into a bowl with the ground pork, salt, soy sauce, and Worcestershire sauce. Combine fully, then form into patties.

Wrap each of the patties tightly in plastic wrap, then aluminum foil. Place them all in a resealable freezer bag and put them in the freezer for at least 1 hour before cooking, up to 1 month.

When you are ready to cook, put a large skillet or Dutch oven on medium heat and add the oil. Heat the oil until it is 330°F to 350°F. If you don't have a thermometer, you can test with a wooden spoon or chopstick—if bubbles form around the spoon or chopstick in the oil, then the oil is hot enough. You don't want it to be boiling or too bubbly here, so try to always check the temperature.

Fry the HAMburgers for 6 to 8 minutes, then turn them over and fry them again for an additional 5 to 6 minutes. If your skillet is not large enough for all the patties, add more oil as needed and fry another batch the same way (making sure to bring the oil back up to temperature). Serve with hamburger buns and condiments as needed.

cinnamon-rosemary pork chops

You might not think a meat with a reputation for being dry makes for a great freezer option. But the pork chop has been given short shrift. This recipe is an exciting pop of flavor—cinnamon and rosemary is a pairing that should be undertaken more. But between the brine, the bone, and the initial sear, this recipe allows for you to just shove the chop in the oven from frozen and pull it out without another thought. I know it seems hard to believe, but with the right forward planning for the brining and searing, you can have pork chops straight from frozen any day of the week.

Serving: 8

Ingredients
½ cup Greek yogurt
¼ cup finely chopped rosemary
2 tablespoons cinnamon
2 tablespoons salt
8 bone-in pork chops
1 tablespoon canola oil

Combine the yogurt, rosemary, cinnamon, and salt in a bowl and mix thoroughly. Coat the pork chops in the cinnamon-rosemary mixture. Let the pork chops sit at least 8 hours or overnight in the fridge to brine in the marinade.

Preheat oven to 400°F if you are planning to eat now. Place an oven-safe pan on the stove on medium-high heat. Once the pan is hot, add the canola oil to the pan, then the pork. Cook for 3 minutes, not moving, until one side has browned.

If You Are Eating Now
Turn the chops over. Move the skillet into the oven and cook for an additional 8 to 15 minutes or until the internal temperature has reached 135°F to 145°F. The cook time depends on the thickness of your pork. Average cook time is about 12 minutes, but if you have particularly thin or thick pork chops, keep that in mind. Also keep in mind that the pork temperature will continue to rise as it rests, so if you want it more on the medium-rare side you should pull it out closer to 135°F. Remove from the oven and let the tenderloin rest for at least 3 minutes before carving.

If You Are Freezing for Later
Remove the pork from the pan and allow it to completely cool to room temperature. Wrap each chop tightly in aluminum foil, then place in a freezer-safe resealable bag or container.

When you are ready to eat, preheat the oven to 400°F. Remove the chops from the container and place them still wrapped in aluminum foil on a sheet pan. Place the sheet pan in the oven and cook for 30 to 45 minutes until the chops are fully cooked or until the internal temperature has reached 135°F to 145°F. Check the temperature because the timing really will depend heavily on the size of your chops. Remove from the oven and let the tenderloin rest for at least 3 minutes before eating.

ginger-honey pork tenderloin

Pork tenderloin is a dish that is easy to make once you know how to steer clear of its pitfalls. Because it is a lean meat, you have to know how to protect it. This recipe calls for a bit of sour cream and honey to give it a nice coating, so it doesn't dry out. What's particularly cool about honey is that it actually never totally freezes, so it creates a nice barrier for your pork. With the additional flavor of the ginger, this dish stays impressive whether you freeze it or not. This dish does well hot or at room temperature, but just don't carve until ready to serve.

Serving: 8–10

Ingredients
3 tablespoons sour cream
2 teaspoons grated ginger
2 tablespoons honey
4 teaspoons salt
4 pounds (2–4 pieces) pork tenderloin
1 tablespoon extra-virgin olive oil

Preheat oven to 400°F if you are planning to eat now. Combine the sour cream, ginger, honey, and salt in a bowl. Coat the pork tenderloin in the ginger-honey mixture. Place an oven-safe pan on the stove on medium-high heat. Once the pan is hot, add the olive oil to the pan, then the tenderloin. Cook for 6 minutes, turning every few minutes so that each side browns.

If You Are Eating Now
Move the skillet into the oven and cook for an additional 10 to 15 minutes or until the internal temperature has reached 145°F. The cook time really depends on the thickness of the meat, so start checking early if you are cooking a smaller cut. Remove from the oven and let the tenderloin rest for at least 3 minutes before carving.

If You Are Freezing for Later
Remove the tenderloin from the pan and allow it to completely cool to room temperature. Wrap each tenderloin tightly in aluminum foil, then place in either a freezer-safe bag or container.

When you are ready to eat, preheat the oven to 400°F. Remove the tenderloin from the container and place it on a sheet pan. Unwrap it from its aluminum foil and flatten it to cook the pork on. Cook for 20 to 25 minutes until it is fully cooked or until the internal temperature has reached 145°F. The cook time really depends on the thickness of the meat, so start checking early if you are cooking a smaller cut. Keep in mind that the thinner your tenderloin, the faster it will cook. Remove from the oven and let the tenderloin rest for at least 3 minutes before carving.

pulled pork and grits

Growing up, I always loved shrimp atop grits with a tomato sauce. Why don't we use this methodology for meat? Cultures that use polenta often have braised meats on top, so this is my combination of both of these ideas. Pulled pork does take some time, but it is one of the few freezer recipes that actually gets better the longer it sits. You can make this without the grits but try and give it all a whirl—it will be worth it for the ease in which you can pull it out in a pinch and serve to a happy crowd.

Serving: 8–12

Ingredients

2 tablespoons kosher salt, divided, plus more as needed

¼ teaspoon cayenne

1 teaspoon freshly ground black pepper

1 teaspoon paprika

1½ teaspoons garlic powder, divided

1 (5–7 pound) boneless pork butt or shoulder

1 tablespoon +1 teaspoon canola oil, divided

3 tablespoons molasses

3 tablespoons + 1 teaspoon Worcestershire sauce, divided

1 cup + 1 tablespoon apple cider vinegar, divided

½ cup brown mustard

1 cup water, plus more as needed

5 cups milk

6 tablespoons unsalted butter

3 cups stone-ground grits

1 large white onion, finely diced

3 cups chopped cherry tomatoes

Preheat the oven to 300°F. Combine 1 tablespoon salt, cayenne, pepper, paprika, and ½ teaspoon garlic powder in a bowl, then rub the pork with the seasoning. Place a large Dutch oven on medium-high heat and add 1 tablespoon oil. Once the oven is hot, add the pork and cook for 5 to 7 minutes, turning occasionally so that the meat browns on all sides. While the meat is cooking, combine the molasses, 3 tablespoons Worcestershire sauce, 1 cup apple cider vinegar, mustard, and water. Add the sauce into the Dutch oven with the pork, cover it, then move it to the oven. Cook for approximately 4 to 5 hours, depending on the size of your pork. When the pork starts to feel tender, remove the cover and place it back in the oven for an additional hour. The meat is done when it rips apart easily.

When the meat is approximately 30 minutes from being done, you can start cooking your grits. Place the milk, butter, and remaining salt in large saucepan on medium-high heat and bring to a boil, watching to ensure it doesn't bubble over. Add the grits and turn the heat down to a low simmer. Stir occasionally until the grits fully come together, about 15 to 20 minutes. Add more water as needed, but just be sure not to overcook the grits. You want them to have a bit of bite, especially if you'll be freezing them.

When the meat is 15 minutes from being done, place a skillet on medium-high heat and add in the remaining canola oil. Add in the diced onion and additional apple cider vinegar along with the additional garlic powder, additional Worcestershire sauce, and a dash of salt and cook for 10 to 12 minutes, or until the onions start to look browned and translucent. Add in the cherry tomatoes and cook for another 3 to 4 minutes, until the cherry tomatoes are still a bit firm but have softened.

If You Are Eating Now

Remove the pork from the oven. Taste it to see if you need more salt or vinegar, then add as needed. Serve by putting the grits on the bottom, the tomato and onion mixture in the middle, and a heaping portion of pork on top.

If You Are Freezing for Later

Remove every element from the heat and allow it all to cool down to room temperature. Break apart the pork and add the tomato and onion mixture to the pork. Freeze the pork and the grits separately, either in freezer-safe containers or resealable bags. Make sure to keep portion sizes in mind so that you can reheat individually if needed.

You can defrost this dish, but it does perfectly well straight from the freezer. When you are ready to eat, place the pork and grits in separate microwave-safe containers (you can combine them if you don't mind stirring them together). Heat them each 1 minute at a time in the microwave, stirring each minute, until both are hot. You can add a bit of water to both as needed to reconstitute. When both are hot, combine in a bowl with the grits on the bottom.

five ingredient, three-hour brisket

I don't know why brisket recipes always seem to take 5 hours and consist of 10 or more ingredients. I love a good slow-cooked piece of meat with a complex rub, but for meals at home we can't always make that work. This recipe aims to dispel the myth that those steps are necessary. You can add more if you want to make this into a full meal—onions, carrots, and other hearty vegetables are a great companion (just be sure to add a bit more liquid to even it out). But with only 5 ingredients and a 3-hour cooking time, this brisket will be the surprise hit of any evening.

Serving: 6–8

Ingredients
3 pounds brisket (preferably a flat cut)
Dash salt, plus more as needed
1 cup pomegranate juice
1½ cups beef stock
1 teaspoon chili flakes
1 cup diced shallots

Preheat the oven to 325°F. Place a Dutch oven or other large pot on the stove on medium-high heat, then salt the brisket on both sides. Add the brisket fat-side down in the pot (if your brisket doesn't have much fat you can add a bit of oil to the bottom of the pot to prevent sticking). Let it cook 3 to 5 minutes on each side until it has browned a bit. Add the pomegranate juice, beef stock, chili flakes, and shallots. Place in the oven, covered tightly. Remove after three hours. If your brisket is a little larger or a little thicker, adjust the cook time accordingly. There should be a little bit of sauce on the bottom that you can spread across the brisket to make it juicier. Test to make sure it is fully cooked and add more salt as needed.

If You Are Eating Now
Serve as is.

If You Are Freezing for Later
Allow the brisket to fully cool down, then break it into individual serving sizes. Freeze in a resealable freezer container or bag of your choosing.

When ready to eat, you can either defrost or cook straight from frozen. You can cook in the microwave or in an oven on 400°F. The timing will depend on the size of the piece you are cooking, so make sure to check as you go. You can add a bit more liquid (even 1 tablespoon or 2 of water will suffice) to get started.

beef enchiladas with salsa verde

NO DEFROSTING

At its core, an enchilada is a Mexican dish that can run the gamut of any corn tortilla stuffed on the inside with a sauce on the outside. This version tries to keep it simple with ground beef that cooks quickly, salsa verde that brings a lot of flavor without a ton of work, and a cheesy topping that no one can refuse.

Serving: 8

Ingredients
1 pound ground beef
1 tablespoon cumin
1 tablespoon chili powder
2 teaspoons salt
2 cups shredded Monterey Jack cheese
1 cup roughly chopped cilantro
1 cup sour cream
2 cups salsa verde, divided
1 (15-ounce) can black beans, drained
16 (6-inch) corn tortillas

In a skillet, brown the ground beef, cumin, chili powder, and salt together for 5 minutes. While the beef is cooking, make the cheese topping: Combine the cheese, cilantro, and sour cream in a bowl. Drain any excess oil from the beef, then add 1 cup salsa verde and the black beans to the beef and take the skillet off the heat. Wrap the tortillas in a wet paper towel, a few at a time, and put them in the microwave for 30 seconds. Dip each tortilla in the remaining salsa verde so that the whole tortilla is moist. Put approximately ¼ cup filling into a line in the center of the tortilla. Be careful not to overfill, as the tortilla can break. Roll the tortilla over the filling, then tuck it in. Place the tortilla on aluminum foil, seam-side down. Continue to roll each enchilada until all are made.

If You Are Eating Now
Preheat the oven to 350°F. Take as many enchiladas as you want to eat now and put them with the aluminum foil down in a casserole dish. Spread the cheese mixture on top and put in the oven for 25 to 30 minutes. Eat hot.

If You Are Freezing for Later
Make sure that each serving is individually wrapped in aluminum foil. Typically, a single serving is 2 tortillas. Spread the cheese mixture on top and carefully wrap the enchiladas in the aluminum foil. Place them in a resealable container or freezer bag and put in the freezer, being careful not to tilt them when they are freezing. When you are ready to cook, preheat the oven to 350°F. Put the enchiladas, still wrapped in the aluminum foil, in a casserole dish. Cook for 40 minutes, then remove the foil (or at least open the foil so that the enchiladas are no longer wrapped) and bake for an additional 5 to 10 minutes.

ground lamb with
mint and pomegranate

Travel can illuminate recipe ideas, but sometimes even other people's trips can serve as inspiration. My father-in-law came back from one of his annual trips to Israel a few years ago and shared a photo he took of a dish he ate with ground lamb on a bed of labneh topped with mint, pistachios, and pomegranates. I had to immediately make my own version and the result is one of my favorite meals. It is quicker to make up front than most meat dishes because the meat is already ground, and it also heats up in a flash. I'm just glad he took the photo.

Serving: 6–8

Ingredients
3 pounds ground lamb
1½ cups pomegranate seeds, divided
2 cups chopped mint, divided
1½ cups shelled unsalted pistachios, divided
3 teaspoons salt
3 teaspoons cumin
1½ cups labneh (or the thickest Greek yogurt you can find), divided

Place a pan on medium-high heat. Combine the lamb, ½ cup pomegranate seeds, 1 cup mint, ½ cup pistachios, salt, cumin, and ¾ cup labneh in a bowl and mix. Place the lamb mixture in the pan and cook, stirring occasionally (it will get easier to stir as it cooks) for about 5 minutes or until it has cooked through.

Remove the lamb from the pan (leaving the excess fat) and stir in the remaining pomegranate seeds, mint, pistachios, and labneh.

If You Are Freezing for Later
Allow the mixture to fully cool down, then place in single-serving freezer-safe containers or bags. Place in the freezer.

When ready to eat, you can either allow the lamb to defrost overnight in the fridge or cook it from frozen. Heat in the microwave, stirring every 30 seconds to 1 minute until hot.

spiced lamb kebabs

Almost every culture in the world has a take on what we most commonly call kebabs. This recipe's Indian-inspired yogurt marinade packs a lot of punch. Because of the size of the cubes of lamb, it will cook quickly, even from frozen, and make for a simple meal no matter the time constraints. A few things to consider: Make sure your lamb weight doesn't include any bones. And keep in mind that it is okay if you are missing a spice or two or need to swap in or out some vegetables. This recipe is meant to be tweaked and can serve as a great spice-cabinet raid. Make a whole batch of these kebabs and serve them whenever you need something a little special but easy.

Serving: 8

Ingredients
3 pounds lamb
1 cup plain yogurt
Juice of 2 lemons
1 teaspoon cumin
1 teaspoon coriander
½ teaspoon turmeric
1 tablespoon grated ginger
2 teaspoons salt
4 zucchinis, sliced into 1-inch pieces
2 large red onions, diced into 1-inch pieces

Equipment
10–15 skewers

Trim off the excess fat from the lamb and cut the meat into 1-inch cubes. If you are using wooden/bamboo kebab sticks, soak them in water for at least 10 minutes (so they don't burn later).

In a bowl, combine the yogurt, lemon juice, cumin, coriander, turmeric, ginger, and salt. Coat the lamb cubes, zucchinis, and onions in the marinade.

Make your kebabs on whatever kebab sticks you have. Alternate the lamb, zucchini, and red onion, filling the sticks almost completely.

If You Are Eating Now
Turn on your oven's broiler and make sure the rack is 4 inches below the top. Broil the kebabs 2 to 4 minutes on each side, depending on how rare you like them.

If You Are Freezing for Later
Place the kebabs on a plate or sheet pan and put in the freezer. Once they are frozen (at least 1 hour) put all the kebabs in a freezer-safe bag or container.

When ready to cook, turn on your oven's broiler and make sure the rack is 4 inches below the top. Broil the kebabs 3 to 5 minutes on each side, depending on how rare you like them.

fish and seafood

spicy clam pizza

This pizza is one of those perfect dishes that feels worthy of guests but somehow also hits the trifecta of quick, easy, and inexpensive to make. The flavor of the clams paired with the spice of the garlic and chili flakes makes for a combination you'll keep reaching for, and the quick preparation here makes it suitable for even the busiest of weeknights. If you have kids around (or just someone who can't take the spice) you can certainly feel free to reduce the chili flakes and garlic, but you might want to increase the Parmesan to add a bit more flavor back in.

Serving: 2 medium pizzas (each serves 2 to 3)

Ingredients

2 pounds (32 ounces) pizza dough

Flour for dusting

½ cup ricotta cheese

1½ cups finely grated Parmesan cheese

6 large garlic cloves

2 (10-ounce) cans clams, drained

1 tablespoon fresh thyme

½ teaspoon chili flakes (Aleppo style preferred)

1 teaspoon salt, plus more as needed

Preheat the oven to 400°F. Cut the pizza dough in half and make two balls. Dust a little flour on your surface, then roll out the doughs with a rolling pin (or your thumbs if you need to!) to your desired crust thickness. Place the two crusts on a pizza stone or sheet pan lined with aluminum foil and put in the oven for 6 minutes. Remove and allow the crusts to cool.

When cool, spread the ricotta evenly across the pizzas, making sure that there is a small amount of space left at the edges. Sprinkle Parmesan cheese on top. Grate the garlic cloves (if you can't grate it all, you can chop the remainder) and sprinkle it across the pizzas. Add the clams, thyme, chili flakes, and salt on top.

If You Are Eating Now

Pop the pizza in the oven for 10 minutes, then remove and serve hot.

If You Are Freezing for Later

Wrap the pizza tightly in plastic wrap, then another layer of aluminum foil. If you have a freezer-safe bag that is large enough, you can use that too. Place in the freezer.

When you are ready to cook, preheat the oven to 400°F. Put the pizza on a pizza stone or lined sheet pan and cook for 15 to 20 minutes, or until the cheese has melted. Remove from the oven and serve hot.

shrimp skewers

Shrimp have always felt to me like perfect little ocean bites. They take on almost any flavor you throw at them, they are quick to cook, and they have a texture that can rival any meat. They also have the distinct advantage of freezing well, but I've had a lot of days where I look in the freezer to find some shrimp for my grits and end up defrosting an entire pile. This recipe aims to solve that shrimp conundrum and make them into an easy, delectable treat that can go straight from the freezer to the oven. By adding the flavor and the cooking device before you freeze, you set yourself up for simplicity down the road. And it's one of the best freezer dishes for serving to guests because they look impressive despite being the simplest items to pop back into the oven straight from frozen.

Serving: 8–10

Ingredients
4–5 pounds medium to large peeled shrimp
1 tablespoon sesame oil
1 tablespoon soy sauce
1 teaspoon salt
1 teaspoon garlic powder

Equipment
10–15 skewers (if using wooden skewers, soak them in water for at least 10 minutes so they don't burn as easily later)

Pat the shrimp dry so that there is no excess liquid. Place them in a bowl and pour the sesame oil, soy sauce, salt, and garlic powder on top. Toss until fully coated. Line two sheet pans with aluminum foil and spray with a nonstick spray. Place the shrimp firmly on the shrimp skewers. The easiest way to ensure they stay on is to skewer them through twice, with the shrimp in a horseshoe shape. Place the skewers on the pans, making sure to have at least a small space between all the shrimp.

If You Are Eating Now
Make sure there is a rack in your oven as close as possible to the top (but where the shrimp and skewers won't burn). Set your oven to broil. Place the shrimp in the oven for 1 to 3 minutes, depending on the size of the shrimp and the distance from the flame. Then, turn them over and repeat. You may want to test with one shrimp before adding them all in to ensure that you are cooking for the correct length of time. Remove from the oven and serve.

If You Are Freezing for Later
Place the shrimp pans in the freezer for at least 1 hour until fully frozen. Then, remove the skewers from the pan and wrap them individually in parchment paper or plastic wrap and place in a large freezer bag, making sure to remove as much air as possible.

When you are ready to cook, preheat the oven by turning on the broiler, making sure the rack is as close as possible to the top. Line and spray another sheet pan and place the skewers on top. Cook the shrimp for 4 to 7 minutes (depending on their size) on one side, then turn the skewers over and repeat. Serve hot from the oven.

the crabbiest crab cakes

Even as a freezer convert, I have to admit that there aren't many foods dramatically improved by using the freezer. But in the case of crab cakes, the freezer actually gives a distinct advantage. I grew up going crabbing, so I understand the benefits and joys of a freshly caught, local crab. But in this recipe, by freezing the crab cake before cooking it, it allows us to use less binding ingredients (fillers like eggs, mayo, and bread crumbs) and instead focus on cramming in as much crab meat as possible. As the crab cooks, the frozen inside doesn't let the cake fall apart and instead you get a golden crispy outside with a juicy inside. I think that's a pretty good trade off. Make these ahead of time, then make an impressive dinner with ease whenever you want.

Serving: 12

Ingredients

2 pounds (32 ounces) jumbo lump crab meat

3 tablespoons (2–3 whole) finely chopped scallions

¼ cup mayonnaise

2 large eggs, beaten

1 tablespoon lemon juice, plus more for serving

½ teaspoon garlic powder

½ teaspoon paprika

1 teaspoon salt

2½ cups Panko bread crumbs, divided

¼ cup vegetable oil, plus more as needed

Lemon wedges, for serving

In a bowl, gently combine the crab, scallions, mayonnaise, eggs, lemon juice, garlic powder, paprika, salt, and 1¼ cups Panko. Form the crab mixture into 1-inch thick patties, like small hamburgers about the size of a baseball (but in a disc shape). Add the remaining Panko to a bowl. Dredge the crab cakes in the Panko so that they are fully coated.

Freeze the crab cakes. You can either place them on a greased sheet pan and let them freeze for at least 1 hour or wrap each of the crab cakes tightly in plastic wrap, then aluminum foil. If you are not cooking them now, put them in a resealable freezer bag and make sure all the air is removed.

When you are ready to cook, put a skillet or Dutch oven on medium heat and add the oil. Heat the oil until it is 330°F to 350°F. If you don't have a thermometer, you can test with a wooden spoon or chopstick. If bubbles form around the spoon or chopstick in the oil, then the oil is hot enough. It should not be boiling. If it is too hot the outside will cook before the frozen part, and if it is too cool the inside will get mushy, so try to always check the temperature.

Fry the crab cakes for 6 to 8 minutes, then turn them over and fry again for an additional 5 to 6 minutes. If your skillet is not large enough for all of the crab cakes, add more oil as needed and fry another batch the same way. Serve hot with lemon wedges on the side.

crab fried rice

Fried rice is filling, packed with flavor, and almost any leftovers can be thrown into it in a pinch. But this recipe has another added element: It can be comforting and delicious even from the freezer. Kicked up flavors like fish sauce, lime, and sriracha make sure it doesn't lose any potency. You could make this dish with any other protein, but I love the ease of crab and the special element it brings to an otherwise pantry-friendly dish.

Serving: 6–8

Ingredients
3 tablespoons vegetable or canola oil, divided
2 large garlic cloves
4 cups cooked jasmine rice
Dash salt
2 eggs
1 bunch scallions, roughly chopped
8 ounces cooked crab meat
2 tablespoons fish sauce
1 tablespoon soy sauce
½ cup cilantro
Juice of 2 limes
1 tablespoon sriracha (optional)

Put a large wok or Dutch oven on high heat and turn on your hood as well. Add 2 tablespoons oil and allow it to heat up.

While the pan is heating, grate the garlic. Add the grated garlic, rice, and salt to the hot pan and stir every 20 to 30 seconds for about 3 minutes.

Move the rice to the side of the pan, add the remaining oil to the pan, and crack the eggs in the center. Scramble them up, allowing them to cook for 1 minute, then fold into the rice. Add the scallions, crab, fish sauce, and soy sauce to the pan and allow to cook for another minute. Remove from the heat, juice the limes on top, and add the cilantro along with any sriracha if you so desire.

If You Are Freezing for Later
Divide the rice into portions and place into freezer-safe containers or bags. Place in the freezer. When you are ready to eat, remove the rice from the fridge and heat in a microwave, stirring every minute or so, until fully hot.

seafood pot pie

Chicken pot pie gets all the attention, but there's a lot to love about a seafood pot pie as well. It feels a bit more decadent without any more work. It's one of the ultimate freezer-to-oven dishes and it's a perfect thing to keep on hand for whenever you need a single dish to serve as an entire meal. You can make it as one big pot pie or in individual portions. Either way, you have an indulgent meal ready to eat at any moment.

Serving: 6–8

Ingredients
1 stick unsalted butter
1 large yellow onion, chopped
5 cups seafood or chicken stock
1 (10-ounce) package frozen peas
2 cups thinly diced carrots
2 cups (2 whole) russet potatoes, diced
¾ cup flour
¼ cup heavy cream
1–2 packages puff pastry, thawed
1 pound shrimp, peeled and cut into bite-sized
 pieces
1 pound halibut or thick white fish, cut into
 cubes
Milk or beaten egg

Preheat oven to 375°F if eating now. Melt the butter in a large saucepan over medium-high heat and add the onion. Cook for 5 to 7 minutes or until the onion starts to soften. Add the stock, peas, carrots, potatoes, flour, and cream. Combine, making sure that there are no clumps of flour. Remove from the heat.

Cut the puff pastry depending on the size of your vessel(s). If you are making individual pies, you may want to buy two packages of puff pastry to make sure you have enough. Add the shrimp and halibut to the saucepan and mix everything together. Fill your vessel(s) with the mixture almost all the way to the top. Add the puff pastry to the top and crimp the edges so that the puff pastry holds to the sides of the vessel(s).

If You Are Eating Now
Brush milk or egg on top, cut a slit in the puff pastry to allow steam to come through, and place on a sheet pan (in case there is spillage), then place in the oven. Cook for 45 minutes to 1 hour, making sure the top has browned. Serve hot.

If You Are Freezing for Later
Cover the vessel(s) with plastic wrap and a layer of aluminum foil, then place in the freezer. When ready to cook, preheat the oven to 375°F. Remove the plastic wrap and foil and place the vessel(s) on top of a sheet pan. Cook for 1 hour or until the pies are fully cooked and the top has browned.

artichoke and olive-crusted fish

Fish is one of the harder foods to freeze if you are lazy like me and really hate defrosting. Some fish are too delicate to handle that kind of cooking, but thin white fish (without a lot of flavor) like perch or tilapia can turn this notion on its head. The texture isn't too affected by freezing, and the tapenade on top is so flavorful that no one will know the difference. The extra bonus is that because these fish are so thin, you don't end up cooking it much longer than a regular piece of fish, so place a few in your freezer and have fish anytime without all the fuss.

Serving: 10

Ingredients
½ cup pitted kalamata olives
1 (14-ounce) can artichoke hearts, drained
1 tablespoon tomato paste
½ teaspoon salt, plus more as needed
2½ pounds (10 pieces) perch or tilapia

Add the olive, artichoke hearts, tomato paste, and salt into a blender and fully blend into a tapenade. If your blender needs a bit more liquid, add a bit of olive oil to help.

If You Are Eating Now
Preheat the oven to 450°F. Line a sheet pan with aluminum foil and grease it. Place the fish on the pan, salt it on both sides, then spoon a heavy layer of tapenade onto each fish, flattening it out so that it covers the whole fish. Place in the oven for 8 to 10 minutes and serve hot.

If You Are Freezing for Later
Place each piece of fish on a piece of greased aluminum foil. Salt it on both sides. Spoon a heavy layer of tapenade onto each fish, then flatten it out so that the whole top of the fish is covered. Carefully wrap each piece of fish in aluminum foil. Make sure to remove all the air without the foil sticking too much to the tapenade. Place all the wrapped fish in a resealable plastic freezer bag, then put in the freezer, making sure to lay flat with the tapenade side up for the first few hours of freezing (you can move them after that).

When you are ready to cook, preheat the oven to 450°F. Unwrap the fish and cook on the same aluminum foil on a sheet pan for 13 minutes, or until cooked all the way through.

kerala-inspired fish curry

India's Southern state Kerala is often referred to as the land of spices, and when I lived in India, I kept finding myself going back. For me, it was like a tropical paradise that came with the best possible food—flavorful seafood dishes infused with fragrant coconut and acidic tamarind along with an array of spices that are grown right nearby. This curry is an homage to those flavors I fell in love with. If you can't find tamarind paste in your local stores, it is easy to purchase online or can be substituted with lime. And this curry goes great with rice, on noodles, or with a hunk of bread. Either way, it's a combination worth savoring.

Serving: 8–10

Ingredients
2 tablespoons ground coriander
2 tablespoons chili powder
¼ cup curry powder
2 teaspoons salt, plus more as needed
½ cup tamarind paste/concentrate (or ½ cup lime juice if you can't find tamarind)
¼ cup coconut oil
12 garlic cloves, diced
2 large onions, diced
4 (13.5-ounce) cans coconut milk
2 pounds thick white fish, cut into 1-inch pieces
Salt to taste
Parsley (optional)

Combine the coriander, chili powder, curry powder, salt, tamarind paste, and coconut oil in a pot on medium-high heat and toast the spices for two minutes. Add the garlic and onions to the spices and cook for 7 more minutes. Add the coconut milk and fish.

If You Are Eating Now
Cover and cook for at least 8 minutes. Taste to see if you want more salt and serve hot, adding parsley on top to garnish if desired.

If You Are Freezing for Later
Remove the pot from the heat, uncovered, and allow to cool down to room temperature. Place the curry in small freezer containers or heavy-duty freezer bags.

When you are ready to eat, this curry can be reheated from frozen in a microwave or on the stove top. In the microwave, cook in 1-minute increments, stirring as you go. On the stove, place on medium heat and stir frequently. (You do not want the block of soup in frozen form to burn on the bottom!) Serve hot and add fresh parsley on top if desired. You can serve with rice, noodles, or bread.

rhubarb-miso salmon

I know it might seem impossible to cook salmon straight from frozen and have it come out well, but this recipe proves that with the right technique almost anything is possible. The secret lies in steaming the fish before roasting it. The other key is the flavorful sauce that provides a barrier to the cold. You could use this sauce on almost anything—plain on some bread, mixed into a salad dressing, or as the topping to almost any protein. And if you can't find rhubarb, strawberry also works great here.

Serving: 8

Ingredients
12 (2 cups) rhubarb stalks, chopped
Drizzle olive oil
½ cup white miso
8 filets (6–8 ounces) salmon
Dash salt

Place a pan on medium-high heat. Place the rhubarb in the pan with olive oil and cook for approximately 5 minutes, or until the rhubarb breaks down and starts to look jammy. When done, place in a bowl with the miso and fully combine. Make sure the rhubarb completely incorporates into the miso.

Sprinkle salt on top of each piece of salmon. Spread the miso rhubarb mixture evenly across each filet, making sure the mixture isn't too hot. If it is, place the bowl in the freezer for 1 or 2 minutes to get it closer to room temperature.

If You Are Eating Now
Preheat the oven to 450°F. Place the filets skin-side down on a parchment-lined sheet pan and put in the oven for 12 to 15 minutes (depending on the size of your salmon), or until the internal temperature has reached 140°F if you like medium rare and 145°F for medium.

If You Are Freezing for Later
To freeze, wrap the fish filets individually in plastic wrap or aluminum foil, then put into a freezer-safe resealable plastic bag, making sure to remove all air. Place in the freezer. When you are ready to cook, heat a nonstick skillet to medium-high heat (if you don't have a nonstick skillet, you can use a bit of olive oil here). Place the fish topside down in the skillet and cook for 4 minutes. Flip it over onto the skin, reduce the heat to medium low, and cover it. Cook for 6 to 12 minutes, or until the fish is cooked through and the internal temperature is 140°F. The cook time depends on the size and type of salmon. Wild salmon often cooks a bit faster than farmed because it is thinner. Serve hot.

ginger-lime halibut

There is a lot of unnecessary bemoaning of frozen fish, but there are plenty of fish that freeze perfectly well (and most grocery store fish was once flash frozen anyway). You want to look for a lean fish because the fattier varieties and very delicate thin ones don't hold up as well. I love the flavor, texture, and hearty nature of halibut here, but this recipe is also interchangeable with cod. The best news is that you can throw this fish straight from frozen onto a pan. And maybe you can even change some minds about frozen fish.

Serving: 8

Ingredients
3 tablespoons ginger
¼ cup almonds
Juice of 3 limes
2 tablespoons soy sauce
Dash salt
8 (6–8 ounce) skin-on halibut filets

Combine the ginger, almonds, lime juice, and soy sauce in a blender and blend until it forms a thin paste. If your blender isn't that strong and it doesn't look like a paste you can always add a bit of oil or water to get it moving. Salt the fish on both sides, then add a thick layer of the ginger-lime paste to the top and sides.

If You Are Eating Now
Preheat the oven to 450°F. Place the fish on a greased sheet pan or aluminum foil. Place the pan in the oven for 12 to 14 minutes, depending on the size of your filets (or until the internal temperature is 140°F). Remove and serve hot.

If You Are Freezing for Later
Freeze each piece of fish individually. You can either wrap each filet in plastic wrap or aluminum foil and place them all in a resealable container or bag or freeze them all on a sheet pan for 1 hour and place in a resealable container or bag (ensuring that as much air is out of the container as possible).

When you are ready to cook, heat a nonstick skillet to medium-high heat (if you don't have a nonstick skillet you can use a bit of olive oil here). Place the fish topside down in the skillet and cook for 4 minutes. Flip it over onto the skin, reduce the heat to medium low, and cover it. Cook for 6 to 12 minutes, or until the fish is cooked through and the internal temperature is 140°F.

crispy fish sticks

Fish sticks are a staple for kids and adults alike, but the healthy base is usually overpowered by a lot of ingredients and bread crumbs that hide the actual fish. This version allows the fish to shine by using Panko (a Japanese version of bread crumbs that are lighter and crisper than other varieties) and no added flour. With only four base ingredients, the flavor of the fish is matched only by the crunchy, golden texture of the Panko.

Serving: 8

Ingredients
4 pounds cod
4 eggs
3 cups Panko
1 teaspoon salt
Vegetable oil as needed

Line a sheet pan with parchment paper. Cut up your cod into sticks. I typically like to cut mine about 1-inch wide, then 3 to 5 inches long. Whisk the eggs in a bowl. In a separate bowl, combine the Panko and salt. Take each piece of cod and dip it in the egg, then roll it into the Panko. Place the fish sticks on the parchment-lined sheet pan and repeat until every piece of fish is coated (you can add a bit more Panko or egg as needed, depending on how you cut up your fish). When you are done, place the fish sticks in the freezer for at least 1 hour or until fully frozen. Transfer them to a freezer-safe resealable bag or container, making sure to remove as much air as possible to store. When you are ready to cook, put a skillet or Dutch oven on medium heat and add the oil. Heat the oil until it is 330°F to 350°F. If you don't have a thermometer, you can test with a wooden spoon or chopstick. If bubbles form around the spoon or chopstick in the oil, then the oil is hot enough. You don't want it to be boiling or too bubbly here, so try to always check the temperature.

Fry the fish sticks for about 4 minutes per side, until golden and cooked through. You should cook them in batches, depending on the size of your pan and how many fish sticks you are cooking at once. Keep in mind that adding fish to the pan will bring the temperature of the oil down, so don't crowd too much. Place the finished fish sticks on a paper towel-lined plate and serve hot.

chapter 8

vegetables and sides

fennel with
clementines and goat cheese

Fennel never tops the list of easy vegetables to make because everyone assumes it needs to be roasted for a long time. But put chopped fennel under a broiler and you suddenly have a meal or side in less than 10 minutes. Combine it with citrusy sweet clementines, the crunch of pepitas, and the creamy tang of goat cheese and you have a dish that still feels alive even after a stint in the freezer. This dish is as easy to heat up in the microwave as it is to make originally, so keep it on hand for a simple lunch or to always have a side dish at the ready.

Serving: 6

Ingredients
2 fennel bulbs
2 tablespoons extra-virgin olive oil
Dash salt
2 clementines, diced into 1-inch cubes
1 cup pepitas (dried pumpkin seeds)
Juice of 1 lemon
1 cup crumbled goat cheese

Turn on your oven's broiler and make sure a rack is close to the top. Remove the fennel fronds (the frilly leaf-like parts growing from the stem) and set aside but keep the stems and bulbs. Chop them both into small 1-inch pieces. Place the fennel on a sheet pan with the olive oil and salt and put in the oven for 6 minutes.

Remove the fennel from the oven and place into a bowl. Allow it to cool, then add all remaining ingredients into the bowl. Combine and serve, if eating now.

If You Are Freezing for Later
Freeze in a resealable freezer bag or container in single-serving increments. When you are ready to eat, microwave the fennel mixture 1 minute at a time, stirring in between, until hot.

soy snap peas

The biggest (and most justifiable) complaint about freezer food is that many blanched and frozen vegetables can be a pretty sad affair once they thaw out. But I was determined to find the loophole in this theory. Enter the pea. If you've opened a bag of formerly frozen peas that you happened to leave on the counter (not saying I ever do that . . .), you might notice they actually don't taste half bad. Peas are made to stand up to the freezer. So too with its cousin the snap pea. Since you would eat this cold either way, there's no additional heat that would degrade the peas. Because of that, the crispness along with the soy help to give the illusion of freshness. This is really one of those recipes that can fully make a freezer convert out of anyone.

Serving: 6–8

Ingredients
2 pounds snap peas, trimmed

1 tablespoon soy sauce

1 tablespoon sesame oil

½ cup finely chopped parsley

½ cup sliced almonds

1 teaspoon salt

Bring a heavily salted pot of water to a boil. Put the snap peas in for just 1 minute, then quickly remove them and put them into an ice bath or run them under cold water until they are cool. Drain them and toss with the soy sauce, sesame oil, parsley, almonds, and salt.

If You Are Freezing for Later
Place the snap peas in a freezer-safe container or resealable freezer bags, making sure to remove as much air as possible. When you want to eat them, remove them at least 12 hours before and allow them to defrost in the fridge. You do not want to reheat these again or they will lose their crispness.

broccoli and cauliflower medley

Cooked vegetables in the freezer often make people wary. There's a fear that they will always come out limp and sad. And while that is definitely true of a lot of vegetables, some of the heartier ones can hold up pretty well as long as they are on the crispier side to begin with. This recipe will hopefully show you how well some vegetables really can handle the freezer.

Serving: 6–8

Ingredients
1½ pounds (1 medium head) cauliflower
2 pounds (3–4 medium stalks) broccoli
3 tablespoons extra-virgin olive oil
Zest and juice of 2 limes
¼ cup fresh chives, chopped
¼ teaspoon cayenne
1 teaspoon garlic powder
1 teaspoon salt

Chop the cauliflower and broccoli into small, bite-sized pieces. They should be roughly chopped and the pieces should be about 1-inch long. Dice the cauliflower a little smaller since it doesn't cook as fast as the broccoli. In a bowl combine them with the olive oil, lime zest and juice, chives, cayenne, garlic powder, and salt. Place the mixture on an aluminum foil-lined sheet pan.

Turn on your oven's broiler, making sure to place one rack as close to the top as possible. Place the sheet pan in the oven for 2 to 5 minutes until the vegetables start to char but not overcook. You'll want to watch them closely; the line between a nice char and a burn can be a matter of 30 seconds. Remove them from the oven. They should be cooked but still very crisp.

If You Are Eating Now

You can eat these as they are if you are a fan of very crisp vegetables. If you like them a little more done, you can set aside whatever amount you want to freeze and stick the rest back in the oven for another couple of minutes to get them a bit softer. Taste and see what you prefer.

(Continued on next page)

If You Are Freezing for Later

Once the vegetables are cooked, let them cool completely to room temperature. Then, place them in freezer containers or resealable bags, making sure to remove as much air as possible and to keep them in individual servings. If you have time for defrosting, you can defrost the vegetables for 12 to 24 hours in the refrigerator before you are ready to cook. Once you are ready, turn on your broiler with the top rack as close as possible to the flame. Place the vegetables on an aluminum foil-lined sheet pan. Cook for 1 to 2 minutes under the broiler until they are hot again.

If you don't have time to defrost, especially if they have been frozen in individual servings, you can cook these straight from frozen in the microwave. Cook for 30 seconds to 1 minute at a time, stirring in between, until hot.

hearty quinoa and beets

Grains and root vegetables are perfect for the wintry conditions of the freezer. Quinoa reanimates without a trace and beets are so solid to begin with that they bear the burden without much fuss. And beets are easier to make than most people think; they just require a bit of forward planning, so plan ahead and make this recipe for a hearty side or main dish.

Serving: 8

Ingredients

6 medium-sized red and/or yellow beets
2 tablespoons balsamic vinegar
2 teaspoons salt, divided, plus more as needed
3 garlic cloves
1 diced medium yellow onion
1 tablespoon extra-virgin olive oil
2 cups water or stock
2 cups quinoa
Juice of 1 lemon
1 cup walnuts

Preheat your oven to 400°F. Cut off the tops of the beets (don't throw those tops away—you can use them later in salads and sautés!). Place the beets individually in aluminum foil along with the balsamic vinegar and 1 teaspoon salt. Wrap them tightly in the foil and place them on a sheet pan in the oven. Cook for 40 to 60 minutes or, depending on the size of your beets, until they are soft when poked with a fork. Remove from the oven and fully cool. When they are cool, peel the skin off using a paper towel; just be careful with red beets not to stain your hands. If you are particularly bothered, you can use gloves here or just leave the skins on, as I often do. Chop the beets into small bite-sized pieces.

Place the garlic, onion, and olive oil in a pot on medium-high heat. Cook for 5 to 7 minutes, or until the onion has started to soften. Add 2 cups water or stock and bring up to a boil. Reduce the heat, add the quinoa, lemon juice, and 1 teaspoon salt and reduce to a low simmer. Cover and cook for 10 to 15 minutes, or however long your quinoa takes to cook.

When the quinoa is done, remove the cover from the pot and fluff. Add the beets in along with the walnuts and combine.

(Continued on next page)

If You Are Eating Now

If eating now, serve hot or at room temperature.

If You Are Freezing for Later

Allow the quinoa to come fully to room temperature. Divide into portions and place in a resealable freezer bag, taking care to flatten out for easier storage and reheating. Place in the freezer.

When you are ready to reheat, place the quinoa in a bowl in the microwave and microwave for 30 seconds to 1 minute at a time, stirring frequently, until the quinoa has come back up to your desired temperature.

cooked kale caesar

When did we decide that Caesar dressing was just for salads? Those timeless flavors can transform even the most boring of lettuce leaves, so why not do the same for cooked greens? The one item that gets lost in the cooking and freezing is that crunch of croutons and crisp lettuce, but adding in some sliced almonds brings the crunch back. Use fresh or frozen kale and you'll find yourself with an easy side dish that adds a ton of flavor without any of the work.

Serving: 4–8

Ingredients
2 pounds fresh or frozen kale
2 garlic cloves, grated
1 teaspoon anchovy paste
Juice of 1 large lemon
2 teaspoons Worcestershire sauce
¼ cup ricotta
1 cup grated Parmesan cheese
½ teaspoon salt, plus more as needed
½ cup sliced almonds

If using fresh kale, bring a pot of water to a boil and blanch the kale by putting it in the water for 2 minutes. Remove and place immediately into an ice bath. Let the kale sit for 1 minute, then remove and dry as much as possible (spreading out a few kitchen towels should do the trick). I like to keep the stems but you can remove them, just be aware that you might need a bit more kale in that case. Roughly chop the kale once you are done drying. If using frozen kale, allow the kale to defrost and spread out on a kitchen towel to dry it as much as possible. Chop it if it does not come chopped.

While the kale is drying, make the dressing. Combine the garlic, anchovy paste, lemon juice, Worcestershire sauce, ricotta, Parmesan, and salt in a large bowl. Put the almonds in a hot dry skillet and toast for 4 to 5 minutes, stirring every minute or so, until they are golden brown. Toss the kale and almonds with the dressing.

If You Are Eating Now
You can eat this at room temperature or put it in the microwave for 1 or 2 minutes, stirring occasionally, until it becomes hot.

If You Are Freezing for Later
Place the kale mixture in single servings in resealable freezer bags or containers, removing as much air as possible. When you are ready to eat, place a portion in the microwave, 30 seconds to 1 minute at a time, stirring in between, until hot.

creamed corn

<30 MINUTES **NO DEFROSTING** **Microwave-FRIENDLY ~~~**

Creamed corn is one of those classics that can get a bad rap when done incorrectly, but it is the perfect freezer food. Fresh corn at its summer peak can be saved for colder months when you want the lush, comforting nature of the creamed version. You can certainly use canned corn here if you like, just make sure to skip the step of cooking the corn. But if you can get your hands on fresh corn, I promise your future self will thank you when it is no longer available, and you have some available in your freezer.

Serving: 4–8

Ingredients
¾ cup heavy cream
½ cup water
4 garlic cloves, chopped
½ teaspoon nutmeg
1 teaspoon salt
8 ears corn
2 tablespoons chopped chives
2 tablespoons yogurt

In a pot on medium heat combine the heavy cream, water, garlic, nutmeg, and salt. Bring to a simmer (be careful not to boil it). Shuck and cut the corn off the ears and add the ears and the corn to the cream mixture. Cook for 5 minutes or until the corn has softened but still has quite a bit of a bite. Remove the pot from the heat, remove the ears of corn, and set aside 2 cups of the corn mixture from the pot. Add the rest of the corn mixture into a blender and blend it fully. Add the blended corn mixture and the reserved corn mixture back to the pot along with the chives and yogurt and stir.

If You Are Eating Now
Cook for 2 more minutes and serve hot.

If You Are Freezing for Later
Allow the corn mixture to fully cool down and divide into freezer-safe resealable containers or bags. Place in the freezer. When you are ready to eat, place the corn in the microwave and cook for 1 minute at a time, stirring in between, until hot.

bean pancakes

Bean pancakes are the ultimate filling food. These savory pancakes are packed with healthy items like beans and oats, but the shallots, garlic, and apple cider vinegar give them an incredible kick that makes them addictive. Grab a few from the freezer and throw them in the microwave for the perfect side accompaniment to a lighter meal, or add a bit of cheese and fresh herbs on top and they can be a meal of their own. They are easy, delectable, and the perfect pinch hitter for any time you need something extra.

Serving: 24 bean pancakes

Ingredients
2 cans black beans, drained
2 shallots
4 garlic cloves
2 eggs
1½ cups rolled oats
2 tablespoons apple cider vinegar
1 teaspoon salt

Optional:
Feta, goat cheese, or sour cream
Cilantro or parsley

Place your griddle or very large nonstick pan on the stove and turn the heat onto medium. While the griddle is coming up to temperature, add the beans, shallots, garlic, eggs, oats, apple cider vinegar, and salt into a blender. Blend fully until the mixture has a batter-like consistency.

Pour pancake-sized circles onto the griddle or pan (you can use butter or oil if desired but it isn't necessary for a nonstick surface). Cook for 2 to 3 minutes, or until the bottom has browned. Flip and cook for 2 to 3 minutes more, until the pancake is cooked but still fluffy in the middle.

If You Are Eating Now
Remove from the griddle or pan and top with crumbled cheese or sour cream and sprigs of an herb like cilantro or parsley.

If You Are Freezing for Later
Remove the pancakes from the griddle or pan and allow to cool completely. Do not stack them on top of each other or they can get soggy. When they are room temperature, freeze them. You can either wrap them individually or freeze on a lined sheet pan for a few hours and throw them all together in a freezer-safe resealable bag.

When you are ready to heat them up, place the pancakes on a plate and heat in a microwave 30 seconds at a time until they are hot. Try not to heat more than 3 or 4 together or they will get soggy. You can top them with crumbled cheese or sour cream and sprigs of an herb like cilantro or parsley.

the most delightful rice

I call this the most delightful rice because it truly lives up to its name: it feels special without being hard to make. It can be made ahead and held for multiple days without feeling stale. It can serve as a simple dinner bowl or as a side to a bigger equation. It travels easily and can fit in at a brunch, picnic, or full dinner party. Whatever scenario you need it for, it delivers, which is why its delight is undeniable.

Serving: 6–8

Ingredients
1 cup apple cider vinegar
¼ cup sugar
1 cup golden raisins
5 cups cooked brown rice (cooled)
1½ cups crumbled feta cheese
1 cup pitted chopped green olives
1 cup quartered green grapes
1 cup chopped walnuts
Dash salt

Place the apple cider vinegar and sugar in a saucepan and bring to a boil, making sure to stir until the sugar has dissolved. Turn off the heat and add the raisins. Let the raisins sit in the liquid for at least an hour (and up to 12 hours, although you might want to refrigerate them after a few hours).

When the raisins are ready drain them fully from the liquid. Combine with the rice, feta, olives, grapes and walnuts. Taste and add salt as needed (feta and olives are salty so depending on your brands you may not need any additional).

If You Are Eating Now
You can eat at room temperature or cook in the microwave for 30 seconds to a minute per portion.

If You Are Freezing for Later
Freeze the rice from room temperature in individual portions in a freezer-safe container or bag, making sure to remove as much air as possible.

When you are ready to eat, heat the rice in a microwave-safe bowl, 1 minute at a time, until hot (stirring in between).

glazed root vegetables

Let the cold weather veggies rule and take a chance with a flavorful glaze. With a honey and molasses coating, along with that delicious flavor of caramelization, you'll have veggies ready anytime. You can certainly substitute here if you want, but only use the heartiest of root vegetables. There's a reason you don't see any squash or potatoes in this recipe, because they tend to get a bit soggier from the freezer. Note: If you don't mind defrosting and want to eat this dish cold on a salad or in a grain bowl, it also can be cooked fully, then defrosted without any additional cooking.

Serving: 8–10

Ingredients
3 tablespoons extra-virgin olive oil
3 tablespoons honey
3 tablespoons molasses
1 tablespoon salt
1 tablespoon garlic powder
3 cups carrots, chopped into 1-inch cubes
3 cups parsnips, chopped into 1-inch cubes
3 cups turnips, chopped into 1-inch cubes

Preheat the oven to 425°F. Line a sheet pan with parchment paper (or grease it in whatever fashion you like). In a large bowl combine the olive oil, honey, molasses, salt, and garlic powder. Add in the carrots, parsnips and turnips and mix all the ingredients well; it will be a bit sticky so make sure that everything is spread very evenly. Place the mixture on top of the sheet pan and put it in the oven.

If You Are Eating Now
Cook for approximately 20 minutes, or until the vegetables have started to brown and are cooked through.

If You Are Freezing for Later
Cook the vegetables for approximately 10 to 15 minutes, or until they are almost cooked but not quite ready to eat. Turn on the broiler for the last 2 to 3 minutes if needed to make sure they have browned. Remove them from the oven and completely cool. Place the vegetables in resealable plastic bags or containers in individual servings so that they can reheat easily. Make sure to remove as much air as possible.

When you are ready to eat, place a portion in the microwave, 30 seconds at a time, stirring in between. They can heat up fast so try not to overcook them. If you placed a very large batch in the freezer you can also heat this up in the oven at 400°F, stirring occasionally, but it is not necessary for smaller batches.

brightened chickpeas with ricotta

This vegetarian dish is quick and filling, yet it still feels vibrant because of the scallions, lemon, and thyme. The subtle creamy ricotta ties everything together no matter how long it has sat in the freezer. Even if you don't have every ingredient, sub in other herbs for thyme; give goat cheese or feta a whirl instead of ricotta; or replace the chickpeas with beans. No matter what, you'll throw together a simple meal that can pay dividends later from the freezer.

Serving: 8

Ingredients
6 scallions, diced
Dash salt
Drizzle extra-virgin olive oil
1 tablespoon thyme
2 cans chickpeas, drained
2 cans artichoke hearts, drained and quartered
Juice of ½ lemon
1 cup ricotta

Place a pan on medium-high heat. Add the scallions, salt, and olive oil to the pan. Cook for 5 minutes or until softened. Add the thyme, chickpeas, artichoke hearts, and lemon juice to the pan and cook for another 3 minutes. Remove from heat and add ricotta.

If You Are Eating Now
You can serve this dish hot or cold.

If You Are Freezing for Later
Allow the dish to cool completely. When cool, separate into individual portions and place in a resealable freezer-safe bag or container and freeze, making sure to remove as much air as possible. When ready to cook, reheat 1 minute at a time, stirring in between, until everything is fully cooked and hot.

mashed potato-stuffed
bell peppers

There are few things most cooks want to emulate less than plane food. But this recipe is actually a riff on a dish that I, surprisingly, once had on a plane. It was simple, hearty, and delicious even though it was reheated in a tiny plane oven. I knew I had to make my own version once I got back on solid ground.

Serving: 8–10

Ingredients
8–10 red, yellow, or orange bell peppers
4 large russet potatoes, peeled and diced
½ cup whole milk
4 tablespoons butter
½ teaspoon onion powder
1 cup chopped scallions
Salt to taste

Bring a pot of water to a boil. Cut the tops off the peppers and de-seed them (making sure not to puncture them in any way beyond cutting the tops off). Add the peppers to the boiling water and cook for 5 minutes, turning occasionally (you can do two batches if you don't have a large enough pot). When they are done, remove from the water and run them under cold water. Set aside. Boil the potatoes for 10 to 15 minutes, or until they are soft and ready for mashing. When they are ready, drain the water and add the milk, butter, and onion powder. Mash until fully combined (you can use a hand blender if you prefer smooth potatoes, but it is not necessary). Add the scallions and salt to your taste. Set aside. When the peppers are cool, peel the skin off (you can easily skip this step if you are pressed for time, but it does add to the texture). Fill the peppers with the mashed potatoes. Salt the outside of the peppers as well.

If You Are Eating Now
Preheat the oven to 400°F. Place the stuffed peppers on a greased sheet pan (or lined with parchment paper) and place in the oven for 20 to 25 minutes. Serve hot.

If You Are Freezing for Later
Make sure the stuffed peppers are completely cool, then place them in a resealable plastic bag and put them in the freezer, making sure to remove as much air as possible. When you are ready to cook, preheat the oven to 400°F. Place the stuffed peppers on a greased sheet pan (or lined with parchment paper) and place in the oven for 30 to 40 minutes. They should be fully cooked through but you can always cook these longer as needed. Serve hot.

israeli couscous with
pecans and apricots

Israeli couscous might be strangely named—it is much more reminiscent of a small pasta than of regular couscous—but I love using it as a counterweight to stronger flavors and textures. Between the strong flavors of the spices, the seemingly endless freshness of the parsley, and the crunch of the pecans, this dish can hold its own.

Serving: 8

Ingredients
3½ cups water or stock

3 cups Israeli couscous

2 teaspoons ground coriander

1 cup parsley, finely chopped

⅔ cup pecans, chopped

1 cup dried apricots, finely chopped

1½ teaspoons salt, plus more as needed

Bring the water or stock to a boil in a pot. Add the couscous and reduce to a simmer. Cook for 8 to 10 minutes until the couscous is just cooked and the water has completely absorbed. Add the coriander, parsley, pecans, apricots, and salt and fully combine.

If You Are Freezing for Later
Allow the couscous to come fully to room temperature. Freeze in individual portions in a freezer-safe container or bag, removing as much air as possible. When you are ready to eat, heat the couscous in a microwave-safe bowl, 1 minute at a time, stirring in between until hot.

rustic eggplant and farro

Eggplant is a perfect vegetable to freeze because the more it is cooked, the softer and more flavorful it becomes, and it melts right into the nutty chewiness of farro, a grain that also can stand up to a bit of freezing. A touch of red wine vinegar adds some zing, and it all combines to make a rustic dish that does well as a main grain bowl or an easy side for a weeknight dinner.

Serving: 4–6

Ingredients

2 small eggplants
1 tablespoon extra-virgin olive oil
1½ cups vegetable or chicken broth
1 cup semi-pearled farro
3 garlic cloves, minced
½ cup slivered almonds
2 tablespoons red wine vinegar
Dash salt

Preheat the oven to 400°F. Cut your eggplants in half lengthwise. Brush the eggplant flesh with olive oil, then place them flesh-side down on a sheet pan. Roast for 30 to 35 minutes, or until the eggplants start to feel soft. Turn on your oven's broiler and cook 1 to 2 minutes more, then flip the eggplants and cook another 1 to 2 minutes. Both sides should be a bit charred but not burned. (You can skip this last browning on either side if you feel that your oven has already browned one part enough.)

While the eggplants are cooking, bring the vegetable or chicken broth to a boil in a pot. Add the farro and garlic, then reduce to a low heat. Cook for 15 to 20 minutes, or until the farro is cooked but still has a bit of texture. When done, remove from heat to cool.

When the eggplants are done cooking, remove them from the oven. Allow the eggplants to cool, then cut them into 1-inch pieces. Add the eggplants, almonds, and red wine vinegar to the farro mixture along with salt to taste.

If You Are Freezing for Later

Place the farro mixture into freezer-safe containers or resealable plastic bags. Try to freeze in individual portions and remove as much air as possible. When you are ready to eat, you can either defrost and serve cold, or you can reheat in the microwave, cooking 1 minute at a time and stirring in between.

citrus-almond couscous

I have always loved the texture of couscous, but I never realized that that texture and size would make it such a great freezer food. Because it never really freezes into a complete solid, couscous unfreezes like a dream. This recipe is packed with flavor, from dual citrus notes to a pairing of spices. This recipe is versatile enough to serve as a party side or reheat for a quick lunch or weekday dinner.

Serving: 6–8

Ingredients
1 tablespoon butter
½ cup chopped shallots
1½ cups chicken or vegetable broth
½ cup freshly squeezed orange juice
1 (10-ounce) box couscous
½ teaspoon salt, plus more as needed
2 teaspoons cumin
2 teaspoons coriander
1½ cups sliced almonds
1 cup chopped parsley
Juice of ½ lemon
Zest of 1 orange

Place a pan on medium-high heat and melt the butter. Add the shallots and cook 4 to 5 minutes until they have started to brown and are a bit translucent. Add the chicken or vegetable broth and orange juice and bring to a boil. Add the couscous, cover, then remove from the heat. Let it sit at least 5 minutes to cook.

If You Are Eating Now
Fluff the couscous with a fork. Add in the remaining ingredients. Stir together and serve warm.

If You Are Freezing for Later
Let the couscous fully cool down. Fluff the couscous with a fork, then add in the remaining ingredients and stir together. Place in a freezer-safe container or resealable plastic freezer bag in individual servings, making sure to remove as much air as possible. Place in the freezer.

When you are ready to eat, add a small dash of water to the couscous (not more than 1 teaspoon per serving) and place in a microwavable container. Put the couscous in the microwave for 1 minute at a time, stirring in between. For a single portion you may not even need more than 1 minute so make sure to watch carefully. Serve warm.

.... chapter 9 ....

desserts

coconut oatmeal cookies

When I was a kid, I used to dread any recipe that had coconut in it, but then I found unsweetened coconut. You get all the essence of real coconut without the processed, sugary flavor of the more common shredded coconuts. And because of the denser ingredients in this cookie, it does particularly well in the freezer. Because they are frozen in individual balls (or a log), anytime you want just a single cookie you can turn on your oven (or toaster oven!) and pop one in. There aren't many things more satisfying than a warm cookie without the work.

Serving: 25–30

Ingredients
1 cup (2 sticks) unsalted butter at room temperature
½ cup granulated sugar
1 cup packed light brown sugar
2 eggs
1 teaspoon vanilla extract
1 teaspoon allspice
1 teaspoon baking soda
1 cup all-purpose flour
1½ cups shredded unsweetened coconut
1 cup chopped walnuts or pecans
2 cups old-fashioned oats

Add the butter, granulated sugar, and brown sugar into a mixer and cream until fluffy (if you don't have a mixer you can do this by hand but really work it hard!). Add the eggs and combine. Then, add the vanilla, allspice, and baking soda and combine. Finally, add the flour and coconut on a low setting until combined. Mix in the nuts and oats by hand until just combined.

If You Are Eating Now
Preheat the oven to 350°F. Grease a sheet pan and add the cookies in spoon-sized balls, ensuring enough space in between so that they can spread out. Bake 12 to 15 minutes or until they have just browned slightly. They will still be soft when you remove them from the oven, but they will harden up as they cool.

If You Are Freezing for Later
You can freeze these in individual dough balls or as a log. For individual balls, scoop them out onto a lined sheet pan and place them in the freezer for at least 2 hours. When they are completely frozen, put them in a resealable bag, ensuring that as much air is out as possible. (I also like to wrap them in parchment paper to give them another layer of protection, but this is optional.) If you'd rather freeze them as a log, roll the dough out into the shape of a long log and wrap it tightly in plastic wrap. Be sure the log is thin enough that when you cut it, each piece will be the size of a cookie. Place the log in resealable

(Continued on next page)

freezer bags and remove as much air as possible. Place in the freezer.

When you are ready to cook, preheat the oven to 350°F. Grease a sheet pan or use parchment paper and remove the dough balls or log from the freezer. Take them out of their wrapping and place them on the sheet pan (if you have a log, cut discs, then place them on the sheet pan). Put the dough in the oven and cook for 14 to16 minutes until the edges have started to brown. They will be soft coming out of the oven, but they will firm up once they cool down.

cherry chocolate cookies

Sometimes you just need a lot of chocolate. This is one of those cookies that doesn't beat around the bush—it is all chocolate, all the time, with a hint of fruit from the dried cherries. This cakey cookie freezes easily and doesn't spread out too much when cooked either fresh or frozen. Think of these as little balls of chocolate delight that can cook straight from the freezer.

Serving: 18–24

Ingredients

12 ounces bittersweet chocolate or baking chocolate between 60% and 70% cacao

8 tablespoons unsalted butter at room temperature

½ cup light brown sugar

½ cup granulated sugar

4 large eggs at room temperature

1½ cups all-purpose flour

½ teaspoon baking soda

⅔ cup unsweetened cocoa powder

½ teaspoon salt

1 cup dried cherries, chopped

Preheat the oven to 350°F if you are cooking now. Break the chocolate into small pieces. Place a saucepan on medium heat and add the chocolate. Stir consistently until it is fully melted. Remove from the heat and set aside.

In a mixer or by hand (if mixing by hand, just make sure to really mix well), combine the butter, brown sugar, and granulated sugar. If using a mixer, beat on a high speed until fluffy. Turn the speed on the mixer down, then add each egg slowly, followed by the chocolate. Be sure at every stage to stop the mixer to scrape down the sides; you want everything fully incorporated but not overmixed.

In a separate, bowl, combine the flour, baking soda, cocoa powder, and salt together. Then, slowly add the flour mixture into the dough, a little bit at a time. Turn the mixer off, then add the dried cherries in and combine carefully.

If You Are Eating Now

Line a sheet pan with parchment paper or nonstick spray. Add the dough in evenly sized balls and bake for 12 to 14 minutes. They will come out soft but will firm up once they cool down.

If You Are Freezing for Later

Freeze these cookies in individual dough balls. Create evenly sized balls and place them onto small individual pieces of plastic wrap. Roll the plastic wrap around each ball, being careful to roll them tightly so that no air remains. Place the wrapped balls in a resealable freezer bag and close, ensuring as much air is removed as possible. Freeze them.

(Continued on next page)

When you are ready to cook, preheat the oven to 350°F. Grease a sheet pan or lay down a piece of parchment paper and remove the dough balls from the freezer. Take them out of their plastic wrap and place them on the sheet pan. Put them in the oven and cook for 14 to 16 minutes until they are slightly hardened. Remove from the oven and cool.

pine nut cookies

This is a version of an Italian cookie so light and simple that it almost seems unfair. And as a bonus, it is gluten-free, so you might make some pickier people happy. Because of its light and airy nature, this cookie can be frozen and defrosted and still seem like a perfect nutty bite. Make these simple, crispy cookies and stash some in your freezer. You'll be ready with a simple dessert anytime. Note: This recipe requires defrosting overnight, so keep the timing in mind.

Serving: 12–16

Ingredients
1 ⅓ cup pine nuts
⅔ cup sugar
2 large egg whites
¼ teaspoon kosher salt

Preheat oven to 325°F and line 2 sheet pans with parchment paper. Blend the pine nuts in a blender, then stir them together with the sugar. Using an electric mixer (or whisk if you have stamina), beat the egg whites and salt in a bowl until they have fluffed up and hold stiff peaks. Gently add in the nut and sugar mixture and combine.

Place small, tablespoon-sized dollops onto the sheet pans, making sure to place the cookies quite far apart (because if they get too big, they spread extra far). Bake the cookies until they are golden, about 11 to 12 minutes. Remove from the oven and allow the cookies to cool on the sheet pans.

If You Are Freezing for Later
Wrap each cookie in plastic wrap, then place them all in a resealable freezer bag. When you are ready to serve the cookies, remove them from the freezer 24 hours in advance and place them in the fridge. Serve when fully defrosted.

·········· four-ingredient flourless ··········
chocolate cake

This recipe is almost so classic that it would seem like the world doesn't need another version, yet most versions don't take the freezer into account—and this is one of the best secret weapons you can have. When I make this cake, I always make at least one extra. It's such a moist cake to start with that freezing it and letting it defrost doesn't change it all that much. You can have your cake and freeze it, too (sorry, but I had to). Keep a version of this cake in your freezer at all times and you'll never be without the perfect crowd-pleasing dessert. Note: This recipe requires defrosting overnight, so keep the timing in mind.

Serving: 1 (9-inch) cake

Ingredients

8 ounces (2 sticks) unsalted high-fat butter, broken into small pieces

8 ounces high-quality dark chocolate, chopped into small pieces

5 large eggs

1 cup granulated sugar

Preheat the oven to 375° F. Grease or line a 9-inch cake pan with parchment paper at the bottom. Melt the butter in a saucepan on a low temperature. Add the chocolate and stir until the chocolate has just melted. Remove the saucepan from the heat and add the eggs one at a time, mixing each one in fully before the next. Add the sugar and combine.

Pour the batter into the pan and bake for 25 to 30 minutes. The cake will look done when the edges seem totally finished and the center is only slightly jiggly. It will set more as it cools. Let it cool completely, then carefully flip it over onto a plate.

If You Are Freezing for Later

Wrap the cake tightly with a few layers of plastic wrap. It's easier to freeze on top of a plate but you could certainly freeze it on its own. If you want to be extra careful, you can also place it in a resealable freezer bag after wrapping it.

When ready to defrost, place the cake in the fridge for at least 24 hours. Remove when ready to serve and top with powdered sugar or any topping you'd like.

spicy brownie thins

Sometimes I'm torn between baking cookies or brownies. What if you want the thinness of a cookie with the fudge interior of a brownie? This is where brownie thins come in. It's like the best of both worlds. But these take it up a notch by adding a little kick to the mixture with a hint of cayenne and a pinch of flaky salt. These can be made ahead and frozen, and because of their thin nature they defrost like a dream. Note: These are not super spicy but if you are worried you can cut the amount of cayenne in half (or even eliminate it).

Serving: 15–20

Ingredients
½ cup all-purpose flour
1 cup granulated sugar
¼ cup dark brown sugar
¾ cup high-quality cocoa powder
3 large eggs
4 tablespoons (½ stick) unsalted butter, melted but cooled
¼ teaspoon cayenne pepper
Pinch flaky salt

Preheat oven to 325°F. Grease and line a rimmed half sheet pan with parchment paper. In a bowl combine the flour, granulated sugar, dark brown sugar, and cocoa powder. In another bowl whisk the eggs together with the butter. Add to the flour mixture and stir together until fully combined.

Spread the brownie mixture onto the parchment-lined half sheet pan. It is a fairly thick mixture, so you may want to use a spatula to help you spread evenly. Also keep in mind that it will spread out when it cooks so it doesn't need to be perfect. Sprinkle the cayenne and salt evenly on top (you don't want chunks, otherwise it will be too concentrated).

Bake for 13 to 15 minutes. The brownie should be firm but not hard, as it will firm up more as it cools. Remove from the oven and allow to cool completely.

If You Are Freezing for Later
Cut the brownies into individual squares and wrap each of them tightly with plastic wrap. Place the brownies in a resealable freezer bag, making sure to remove as much air as possible. When ready to defrost, place the brownies in the fridge for at least 24 hours.

chocolate-covered
frozen banana chips
with sea salt

I love desserts that can also double as a snack. I like to keep a batch of these in my freezer at all times for when I'm jonesing for a quick chocolate fix. The final touch of sea salt is what really takes these little treats over the top by balancing the sweetness and making a kid-friendly dessert feel a bit readier for adults.

Serving: 40–50 banana chips

Ingredients
2–5 ripe but still firm large bananas
2 cups chocolate chips (dark or milk, to your preference)
2 tablespoons canola or coconut oil
2 teaspoons flaky sea salt

Cut the bananas into slices, at least 1-inch thick, depending on your preference. Set aside. Melt the chocolate chips in the microwave, 20 seconds at a time, stirring each time until smooth. You can cook the chocolate in a double boiler or saucepan but I find that the microwave has the least chance of burning and won't get quite as hot. Add in the oil and stir to combine.

Line a sheet pan (or pans that will fit in your freezer) with parchment paper. Using a fork dip each piece of banana into the chocolate, then carefully slide it onto the parchment paper. Sprinkle each piece with a bit of sea salt. Place the bananas in the freezer for at least 1 hour, up to 12 hours. After this time, you can transfer them to a freezer-safe resealable plastic bag where they will hold for up to 1 month. If you are holding them for longer than a few days, I like to wrap them in parchment paper, then place them in the bag, ensuring that as much air as possible has been released. To serve, remove them from the freezer and try to eat within 30 minutes. These bananas do great with almost any small topping: chopped nuts, sprinkles, cocoa powder, graham cracker crumbs, etc. As long as they are small enough to adhere to the chocolate, let your imagination run wild.

pistachio semifreddo
with raspberries

What if I told you that you could make ice cream at home in 20 minutes without an ice cream machine? Welcome to the semifreddo. It's an Italian dessert that is similar to ice cream but with more of a frozen mousse texture. And the bonus is that it needs no cooking and no special equipment. Make it ahead, pull it out of the freezer, and find yourself with a dessert that people will take seconds (or thirds) of. Note: the egg whites are not cooked, so make sure you are using high quality, pasteurized eggs.

Serving: 8–10

Ingredients
1 cup raspberries
½ cup honey
½ cup sugar
1 cup pistachios
6 large egg whites
2 cups (1 pint) heavy cream

Put plastic wrap in a cake tin of any shape or size, making sure to get it evenly in the corners and with a lot of excess hanging off the sides. In a bowl add the raspberries and press them with the back of a spoon to combine. Add the honey and stir together until it forms a paste-like consistency. In a blender or food processor combine the sugar and pistachios and pulse until ground, but with some chunks still left. In a bowl beat the egg whites at medium speed until they have fluffed up with stiff peaks. Set aside, then beat the heavy cream until it has also fluffed up. Very gently, fold the egg whites into the heavy cream, then the sugar-pistachio mixture.

Pour half of the raspberry mixture into the cake tin, then pour half of the egg white mixture on top. Then, pour another layer of the raspberry mixture followed by the rest of the egg white mixture on top. Put the excess plastic wrap on top to cover. Place in the freezer for at least 4 hours, up to 1 week before serving (because of the texture of the egg whites, do not keep it longer).

When ready to serve, remove from the freezer and carefully remove the plastic wrap. Turn over and serve immediately.

vegan chocolate-avocado
ice cream

Putting the words vegan and dessert together can make some people shudder with disdain. But if you can make an ice cream that is as delicious as it is healthy, you might surprise even the most die-hard dessert fans. Try not to hold this ice cream for more than a few weeks, since it really is just fruit, but it makes for an excellent healthy dessert straight from the freezer.

Serving: 6

Ingredients
4 ripe avocados
4 ripe bananas
²/₃ cup cocoa powder
½ cup maple syrup
2 teaspoons vanilla extract

Fully combine the avocados, bananas, cocoa powder, maple syrup, and vanilla together. You can combine with a blender, mixer on a low speed, or even a masher if everything is ripe enough. Place in the freezer, stirring every 20 minutes until the ice cream is completely frozen (about 2 to 3 hours) or freeze it using the settings of an ice cream maker. Keep in the freezer until ready to serve.

If you want to serve this ice cream in individual portions, you can scoop it into halved avocado shells. It makes for a nice serving presentation—just make sure to do it after it has been fully stirred.

two-ingredient magic sorbet

I don't use the word magic lightly. But as someone addicted to both ice cream and fruit, I am always on the hunt for the perfect sorbet—one that tastes just like peak season fruit but is somehow creamy, scoopable, and not icy. It never seemed possible to make at home, especially without an ice cream maker of some sort, but then I found dextrose and it truly did feel like magic. Dextrose is a corn-based sweetener with the same chemical makeup as glucose, or blood sugar, meaning your body metabolizes it easily (unlike fructose, the part of sugar we typically have issues with). Dextrose is ¾ as sweet as regular sugar and its freezing point is twice as low as water. And you can find it easily online. What does this mean? We can make our ice cream less sweet while making it softer and more scoopable, even without an ice cream maker. Hence, the magic.

. . . .

Serving: 6–8

Ingredients
2½ cups pureed fruit
⅓ cup dextrose

If using an ice cream maker, fully combine the fruit and the dextrose, then add to your ice cream maker and follow its instructions to freeze. If you do not have an ice cream maker, put your ice cream in the freezer and stir rigorously every 20 to 30 minutes until it reaches the consistency of ice cream.

berry yogurt popsicles

For anyone who doesn't have an ice cream maker (and doesn't want to bother with one), simple popsicles can be just the trick. I love to make these for my kids because they taste like dessert, but they don't contain any sugar so they can be eaten at any time of day. If you want to add sugar you certainly can, but I love having a sweet treat that is also unequivocally healthy. And I especially love watching something so easy turn into something so delicious.

Serving: 6–8

Ingredients
2 pints berries (a little over 1 cup when pureed)

½ cup Greek yogurt

Blend the berries and yogurt together. Pour into a popsicle mold and add popsicle sticks. If you don't have a popsicle mold, you can use small yogurt cups or other small plastic containers instead and it also works great. Freeze for at least 24 hours. Remove the popsicles from the mold or plastic cups. If they are a little too stuck you can run a bit of warm water on the mold to help loosen them up a bit. Eat straight from frozen.

breakfast

from-frozen french toast sticks

There are a few breakfast items that always feel like special treats because of the mess and sugar they bring into your life. French toast is certainly in that category. But if you could have French toast more easily than a bowl of cereal, why wouldn't you go for it? Well, now you can. French toast sticks can freeze easily and be popped into a microwave for 30 seconds to deliver a quick breakfast. Use the fluffiest bread you can find and make yourself a treat.

· ·

Serving: 6–8

Ingredients

1 cup heavy cream

2 large eggs

¼ cup granulated sugar

½ teaspoon ground cinnamon

½ teaspoon salt

1 large bread loaf, preferably challah or brioche

Preheat the oven to 400°F. In a bowl, whisk the cream, eggs, sugar, cinnamon, and salt. Slice the bread into roughly 1-inch slices, then cut each slice into long sticks (the sizing is up to you, it will all cook the same in the end). Put parchment paper on two sheet pans. Dip each stick of bread into the egg mixture and place on the sheet pan, ensuring a small amount of space between each stick. Put the sticks into the oven for 12 to 15 minutes or until golden and cooked, turning halfway through.

· ·

If You Are Freezing for Later

Allow the French toast sticks to completely cool (you can even use a cooling rack if you have one). Place the cooled sticks into a resealable freezer bag, making sure as much air is removed as possible, and put them in the freezer.

When you are ready to eat, place the sticks in the microwave and cook them 30 seconds at a time until they are hot. If you are reheating a lot of them, and care a lot about the sticks' crispiness, you can put them in a 350°F oven for 5 minutes or so.

mini scones

There are few recipes I make as much as scones. In my last year of college my roommates and I even had a designated afternoon "scone time," where I would bake some scones and we would have a cup of tea and discuss our day. (Before scone time we had an "afternoon drinking society," so the evolution to scones was probably necessary!) They are the perfect little item. The dough freezes like a dream and you can bake just one or an entire batch at a time. Always keep some scones on hand in case you need an afternoon catch-up.

Serving: 16

Ingredients

1½ cups all-purpose flour, plus more as needed

1 cup oats

1 tablespoon baking powder

½ cup sugar

½ teaspoon salt

1 cup heavy cream

1 egg

1 teaspoon vanilla extract

6 tablespoons unsalted cold butter

1 cup small blueberries, fresh or frozen

Combine the flour, oats, baking powder, sugar, and salt in a bowl. In another bowl combine the cream, egg, and vanilla. Grate the butter into the flour mixture and combine. You can use your hands to really get in there but try to be light, so the butter doesn't all melt. Carefully toss the blueberries into the flour mixture, then gently add the wet ingredients. Mix until the dough just comes together.

Sprinkle flour on a surface. Take half the dough and form it into a ball, then flatten it out. Cut the circle in half, then quarters, then eighths. You should have eight small scones. Repeat with the remaining dough.

If You Are Eating Now

Preheat oven to 400°F and cook for 15 minutes on a sheet pan lined with parchment paper.

If You Are Freezing for Later

Put the already cut scones in the freezer on a sheet pan lined with parchment paper (making sure they are not touching). After 1 hour, transfer to a freezer-safe bag or container with parchment paper between each scone, making sure to remove as much air as possible. When ready to cook, preheat the oven to 400°F, take one or more scones out, and cook for 15 to 18 minutes on a sheet pan lined with parchment paper.

·········· ham, egg, and cheese ··········
breakfast sandwich

A lot of breakfast sandwiches have you cooking every part separately. It might look prettier, but these are not sandwiches for show. These are supposed to make life simpler and give you a quick breakfast on the go. You can't beat a ham, egg, and cheese with an easier twist.

Serving: 6

Ingredients

1 tablespoon extra-virgin olive oil
10 eggs, beaten
½ cup of milk
1 teaspoon salt
1 teaspoon garlic powder
1 cup grated sharp cheddar cheese, divided
6 English muffins, halved
½ pound ham, chopped

Preheat the oven to 350°F and place a large skillet on medium heat with the olive oil. Whisk the eggs, milk, salt, and garlic powder together and add to the skillet. Cook for 5 minutes, stirring occasionally. Place in the oven for an additional 10 minutes, or until the eggs have fully cooked through. Remove and sprinkle ½ cup cheese on top. Set aside to cool.

When cooled, cut the eggs into six parts, then place each part on top of an English Muffin half (you can pre-toast your English muffin halves if you like them a bit crispier). Sprinkle the remaining cheese and the ham on top, then place the other half on top of each English muffin to form a sandwich.

If You Are Freezing for Later

Individually wrap each sandwich in plastic wrap, then place in a resealable plastic bag or aluminum foil. Just make sure to remove as much air as possible. Place in the freezer. To heat them up, place the sandwiches in the microwave for 90 seconds. Eat hot.

orange blender loaf

Microwave-FRIENDLY

What if you could just throw everything into a blender and be done? That's basically the concept of this loaf. Take everything but the kitchen sink, including an orange peel, and throw it into the oven. Don't worry about the peel. It gives this loaf a nice bitter note that balances perfectly with the rest of the ingredients. You don't need a mixer, and because of the olive oil, it freezes like a dream. What else could you want?

Serving: 6–8

Ingredients
4 clementines or tangerines (or any thin skinned, seedless variety)

½ cup granulated sugar

¼ cup brown sugar

3 eggs, beaten

⅔ cup extra-virgin olive oil

1¾ cups all-purpose flour

2 teaspoons baking powder

½ teaspoon salt

Preheat your oven to 350°F and grease a baking tin or muffin tins. In a blender fully combine the clementines, granulated sugar, and brown sugar. Pour into a bowl and add the eggs and olive oil and combine. Add the flour, baking powder, and salt and carefully stir until fully combined. Add the mixture to the baking tin or muffin tins.

Place in the oven and cook for 45 minutes (less if making muffins) or until the cake is fully baked through.

If You Are Freezing for Later
Freeze the whole loaf, then defrost in the fridge fully.

lemon-ginger oatmeal

There is no comparison between quick microwave oatmeal and the steel-cut variety, but the amount of time needed to make the latter makes it nearly impossible to have on a consistent basis. Luckily, the freezer is the perfect solution. Make a big batch of oatmeal, freeze it into portions, then heat a portion up for 1 to 2 minutes in the microwave when you want a quick and healthy breakfast. I like this particular flavor combination, but as long as you follow the basic oatmeal directions you can jazz it up however you like.

Serving: 6

Ingredients
4½ cups water or milk
2 cups steel-cut oatmeal
2 teaspoons grated ginger
Juice of 1 lemon
2 tablespoons honey
1 cup blueberries (optional)
1 cup slivered almonds (optional)

Bring the water or milk to a boil in a pot. Add the oatmeal, ginger, lemon, and honey and cook according to package instructions (some oat brands cook in 5 to 7 minutes while others take over 30 minutes), stirring occasionally. When your oatmeal is done but still has a bit of bite, remove it from the stove and stir in the blueberries and almonds if desired.

If You Are Freezing for Later
Grease a muffin tin. Put the oatmeal in the tin and place it in the freezer. Allow the oatmeal to freeze (at least 2 hours), then remove from the muffin tin and place in a resealable freezer-safe container or bag. The individual portions are so important here because they will allow the oatmeal to be easily cooked straight from frozen, so avoid one giant block even if you have multiple people eating!

When you are ready to eat, remove one of the oatmeal blocks and put it in a bowl. Add a teaspoon or so of water or milk and place in the microwave, 1 minute at a time, stirring in between until it is ready to eat.

salmon potato pancakes

There is something undeniable about potatoes cooked with a soft interior and a crispy exterior. I grew up with them in the form of potato latkes, but I have come across so many versions in my travels, from the simple Swiss Rösti to the eggy Spanish Tortilla Española. This version utilizes the freezer to make a whole different offshoot. Freezing the potatoes helps avoid using too much egg or flour as a binder; and adding in a bit of salmon and cream cheese makes for one of the most perfect combinations.

Serving: 16 potato pancakes

Ingredients
4 eggs

¼ cup (2 ounces) cream cheese at room temperature

1½ teaspoons salt

4 cups (16 ounces) grated potatoes, fresh or frozen

8 ounces smoked salmon, chopped

Canola or vegetable oil as needed

Chopped parsley and pepper as needed

Whisk the eggs, cream cheese, and salt in a small bowl. Combine with the potatoes and salmon. Line a sheet pan with parchment paper. Using a large spoon (and preferably your hands!), create pancake-sized balls of the potato mixture and flatten them onto the sheet pan. They don't need to be fully cohesive (they will get more structure by being frozen), but you do want to press them together enough so that they stay together on the pan. Make as many of the pancakes as you can, then put them in the freezer.

After they have been in the freezer for at least 2 hours, you can remove the frozen pancakes from the sheet pan and place them into a freezer-safe container or resealable bag. Make sure to remove as much air as possible from the bag.

When you are ready to cook, put enough oil into a pan to reach ½-inch full. Heat it on medium high or until the oil is hot but not bubbling. (If you place a wooden spoon or chopstick in the oil you should see it bubble around it, but you don't want it to get so hot that it is bubbling independently.) Add as many pancakes as you want to cook, keeping in mind that the larger the batch, the more the oil will cool down as the pancakes enter the pan. Cook for 3 minutes or until brown and crispy on one side, then flip and cook for another 3 minutes. Serve hot, adding parsley and pepper on top as desired.

brussels sprouts hash

<30 MINUTES   **NO DEFROSTING**   **Microwave-FRIENDLY ~~~**

One of the most comforting breakfast foods to me is potato hash. It's the perfect food to warm up a cold day without a lot of effort. This version makes you feel a little less guilty about all that potato and meat with the addition of some Brussels sprouts. Don't be wary if they aren't your favorite—the Brussels here add just a bit of heft and earthiness to the dish. This dish is also versatile enough to be a dinner side if you need something to round out your meal.

Serving: 6–8

Ingredients
3 tablespoons vegetable oil
3 russet potatoes, diced into ½-inch pieces
Dash salt, plus more as needed
5 cups shaved Brussels sprouts
1 cup diced pancetta
½ teaspoon chili flakes
2 tablespoons sherry vinegar
Drizzle balsamic (optional)

Put a wide-brimmed pan on high heat and add the oil. When it is hot, add the potatoes and salt and cook for 5 to 7 minutes, until the potatoes have browned and are almost fully cooked. Set them aside to cool. Combine the potatoes with the Brussels, pancetta, chili flakes, and sherry vinegar and place on a sheet pan (you might need two, so divide as needed). Add salt as needed.

If You Are Eating Now
Turn on the broiler, making sure the top rack is on the highest setting. Put the potato mixture in the oven for 4 to 7 minutes, or until the Brussels sprouts are cooked. Stir halfway through. Serve alone or with a drizzle of balsamic on top.

If You Are Freezing for Later
Turn on the broiler, making sure the top rack is on the highest setting. Put the potato mixture in the oven for 3 to 5 minutes, or until the Brussels sprouts are almost cooked. Set aside to fully cool down to room temperature. Place the Brussels sprouts mixture into a freezer-safe container or resealable bag. Make sure you are making individual servings and try to keep them as flat as possible so that they are easier to heat up later. When you are ready to cook, you can either microwave the contents or place them in the oven. If using the microwave, the dish will be easier to heat up but less crispy. Just place the hash in a bowl and microwave for 1 minute at a time, stirring throughout. If you want the dish to be a bit crispier, turn on the oven to 400°F. Place the hash in an oven-safe pan and put it in the oven for 5 minutes. Turn on the broiler and cook for an additional 3 to 5 minutes, or until the hash is cooked, stirring halfway through. Serve alone or with a drizzle of balsamic on top.

everything biscuits

Everything seasoning packs so much flavor that when paired with the lightness of a biscuit it feels like such an obvious combination. You can make these biscuits square if it's easier for you but I think they are a little bit fluffier when nestled together in a circle—the way I learned the base biscuit recipe from the renowned Southern author Nathalie Dupree. Either way, these biscuits are as easy as can be, resulting in your dough being ready in under 15 minutes. How's that for a breakfast treat?

Serving: 20

Ingredients

1 tablespoon sesame seeds

1 tablespoon poppy seeds

2 teaspoons garlic powder

2 teaspoons onion powder

1 teaspoon salt

4 cups self-rising flour, plus more as needed (White Lily preferred)

2 cups heavy cream, plus more as needed

Preheat the oven to 450°F if you are eating now. In a small bowl combine the sesame seeds, poppy seeds, garlic powder, onion powder, and salt. In another bowl, whisk the flour to break up all clumps, then create a well in the center. Add the cream and very gently bring it all together. Move half the dough to a flat surface (a foldable cutting board is great but your counter is fine). Using another flat surface dusted with a bit of extra flour (the other side of the foldable cutting board or a regular one) press down gently onto the dough until it is about ½-inch thick and even, roughly like a rectangle. You want to work the dough as little as possible. Cut the dough in half and sprinkle some of the "everything" mixture onto the first half of the dough. Fold the other half of the dough on top of the other, creating two layers. Brush a little bit of extra cream on top, sprinkle more of the everything mixture on top, and gently press. You should have a two-layer biscuit dough that has a middle and top layer of "everything" seasoning.

Using a 2- or 3-inch biscuit cutter (or small glass) cut out the biscuits into a circle shape. You may have to press out and fold over the dough again for the second round but be careful not to overwork as much as possible.

(Continued on next page)

If You Are Eating Now

Place the biscuits into a circular cake pan(s) until they are all nestled together, packed in fairly tightly (and, no, you don't need to grease the pan(s)!). If you are making all the biscuits, you might want 2 or 3 pans. Place the pan(s) in the oven for 10 to 12 minutes, or until the biscuits are fluffy. They will still be pale so don't wait for them to brown or you will overcook them. Remove and immediately dump out the biscuits onto the counter and spread them out so that they don't steam each other.

If You Are Freezing for Later

You can freeze the dough either by wrapping each cut biscuit in plastic wrap, or by placing them on a sheet pan with parchment paper and freezing completely. Either way, transfer the biscuits to a resealable plastic bag, making sure to remove as much air as possible.

When ready to cook, preheat the oven to 450°F. Place the biscuits into a circular cake pan until they are all nestled together, packed in as tightly as possible even though they are frozen and won't have as much flexibility (and, no, you don't need to grease the pan!). Bake for 13 to 16 minutes, or until they are fluffy and just starting to look a touch golden (they will still remain very pale). Remove and immediately dump out the biscuits onto the counter and spread them out so that they don't steam each other.

mini veggie frittatas

If you need an on-the-go snack or breakfast, these mini frittatas are a lifesaver. Make a bunch in one go and heat them up in less than a minute if you need something quick. They are the perfect item to always have on hand because they are healthy, easy, and the right size for a small snack. If you want to use them as a meal, just heat up a few and you're good to go. Having a hot breakfast has never been so simple.

Serving: 24 veggie frittatas

Ingredients
16 large eggs
½ cup milk
½ cup grated Parmesan cheese
2 teaspoons salt
1 large zucchini, chopped
1 red, orange, or yellow bell pepper, diced
1 cup sliced cherry tomatoes
¼ cup chopped parsley

Preheat the oven to 400°F. Grease or line a muffin tin with liners. Combine the eggs in a bowl until scrambled. Add the milk, cheese, salt, zucchini, pepper, cherry tomatoes, and parsley and combine. Ladle the mixture into each tin. Place in the oven and bake for 20 to 25 minutes or until the frittatas are set.

If You Are Freezing for Later

Allow the frittatas to cool completely. Place in a freezer-safe container or resealable plastic bag and remove as much air as possible. Place the frittatas in the freezer.

When you are ready to eat, microwave them straight from frozen. You only need 45 seconds to 1 minute if you are heating up a single serving. If you want to heat more, make sure to test their cook time in your microwave first, since you really don't want to overcook these.

sauces, spices, and crust

freezer jam

For a lot of people jam feels like something "real cooks" do. It feels complicated. I would really love to change that perception because I actually think few things are as foolproof and easy as jam. Every batch is meant to be different; it can be sweet or sour; it can be loose or thick; it can be as quick as throwing some fruit in a pot. One thing that can actually make it a little more complex is canning it, so why not just do freezer jam? You can make an easy, rustic jam and throw it right in the freezer to keep the taste of summer (or fall, depending on what you make) all year long.

. . . .

Serving: 1 cup

Ingredients

5 cups fresh berries (blueberries, raspberries, blackberries, or cut strawberries), grapes, or cut stone fruits (peaches, apricots, nectarines, cherries, or plums)

½ cup granulated sugar or more as desired

Juice of ½ lemon

Pinch salt

Put a spoon in the freezer. Place a saucepan on medium heat and add in the fruit, sugar, lemon juice, and salt. Stir frequently until it becomes runnier, so it doesn't stick to the bottom. Bring it up to a low boil and continue to stir occasionally. You will see a bit of foam as it cooks, but eventually that will diminish. When the fruit starts to look jam-like and thick, usually after about 20 minutes or so, test it to see if it is set. To test, take the spoon from the freezer and drizzle a few drops of jam onto it. Wait a few seconds and, using your finger, touch the jam. If it has firmed up into a jam-like consistency, it is done. If it is still loose and runny, you may want to cook it a little bit longer and test again a few minutes later. Depending on how watery your fruit is, you could be cooking up to 30 or even 40 minutes, so don't worry if it seems to take a bit longer than you are expecting. The jam should be about ⅓ of the original mixture once it has reduced properly.

Let the jam cool completely.

. . . .

If You Are Freezing for Later

Put the jam into a storage container or a few small storage containers, making sure to leave ½-inch of room at the top of the container since the liquid will expand when it freezes. Freeze for up to 6 months. To use, place the jam in the fridge overnight and let it defrost completely.

the world's easiest chicken stock

Every time I tell someone I am pulling out stock from my freezer, there's always a comment about how I am so fancy. But stock is the opposite of fancy! You don't need any skill to make a basic stock. It's essentially just throwing bones in water and simmering them. You can add more flavors into whatever you are making with the stock, but as a base, this is all you need. This same technique applies to beef and seafood, but I think chicken is the simplest place to start because it's essentially foolproof. Get into the habit of making a stock out of your chicken bones and you'll always have flavor ready to go inside your freezer.

Serving: 4–8

Ingredients

Leftover bones from a cooked or raw chicken
  carcass

Leftover vegetable peels or tops (onions,
  carrots, celery, garlic, etc.) (optional)

Leftover herbs (thyme, sage, parsley, chives,
  etc.) (optional)

Dash salt

Dash pepper

Put the leftover bones into a large pot along with any vegetables and herbs you want to include. Cover with water and add in a dash of salt and pepper. Bring to a boil, then reduce the heat to a low simmer and cover the pot. Cook the stock for around 2 hours. Strain the stock when finished (if it is cloudy, don't worry—cloudy means flavor!) and freeze in portions.

When you are ready to use the stock, you can either defrost it overnight in the fridge or heat it up from frozen in the microwave, cooking for 1 or 2 minutes at a time, stirring in between.

avocado mash

A plain avocado is just about the worst possible item to freeze because that glorious silky texture gets ruined by the icy freezer. But avocado mash is another story: when avocado mixes with lemon, the citric acid dramatically slows down the pace of browning. There are a few other very important elements here: just like in the unfrozen world, air is the enemy of an avocado, so make sure you have squeezed out every last drop. Also remember that a not-so-fresh avocado pre-freeze will certainly not improve in the freezer. You need a just-ripe avocado with no browning to really pull this off. But when you do, you can suddenly have instant guacamole, add a healthy creaminess to your tuna or chicken salad, or make a simple but inspiring avocado toast.

Serving: 5 cups

Ingredients
4 just-ripe avocados
Juice of 2 lemons

Pit the avocados and remove the flesh from the skins. Combine the avocados and lemon juice in a bowl and mash together. Add to a freezer-safe bag and squeeze out every possible bit of air. I like to portion this out into roughly ½ avocado per bag, since that is the best amount for avocado toast, but if you are going to use this for something larger (like guacamole), you can freeze it all together. Place in the freezer. When you are ready to eat, defrost your avocado(s) on the counter or in the fridge. Eat once defrosted.

many-herb pesto

Traditional pesto comes from the Ligurian region of Italy and consists of garlic, pine nuts, basil, and Parmigiano-Reggiano blended with olive oil. For me, it might represent one of the most perfect sauces in the world when done correctly, but its structure is tantalizingly ready to be adjusted. The garlic, cheese, and olive oil base is the quintessential supporting act for highlighting almost any leafy herb or nut. Once you start combining them (often, for me, based on whatever leftovers I have around my house), no two sauces are the same. Pesto also holds beautifully in the freezer. It is a burst of flavor ready to be thrown as a frozen cube into a hot pasta or on a rice bowl that within moments infuses everything. Keep pesto on hand and you'll always have a meal ready to go.

Serving: 4–8

Ingredients
2 garlic cloves
½ cup nuts (pine nuts, almonds, walnuts, etc.)
2 cups mixed leafy herbs (basil, mint, chives, parsley, sage, tarragon, cilantro, etc.)
Dash salt
Dash pepper
½ cup extra-virgin olive oil, plus more as needed
¼ cup Parmesan or pecorino cheese

Combine the garlic, nuts, herbs, salt, and pepper in a blender. As it is blending, slowly drizzle in the olive oil. When it has fully combined, add the cheese and blend a bit more. You can always add more olive oil as needed to get the consistency you are looking for.

Freeze the pesto in small portions—I think an ice cube tray is best. When you are ready to use the pesto, you can either defrost it in the fridge overnight, put a few cubes in a microwave-safe bowl and heat until it has unfrozen, or throw a frozen cube into a dish as it cooks and allow it to defrost in the pot.

za'atar spice blend

I started using za'atar many years ago when my Israeli mother-in-law introduced me to it, but every country, region, and family has their own version. This is mine. I love the toasted sesame combined with the zing of sumac. I like to double or even quadruple this recipe to always have some on hand. It's amazing what can be improved with a little bit of za'atar. Meats, vegetables, salads, even just toast with butter can be transformed by just a sprinkle. And by keeping it in the freezer, you don't have to worry about it losing its potency.

Serving: ¼ cup

Ingredients
1 tablespoon sesame seeds
1 tablespoon thyme, finely chopped
1 tablespoon sumac
1 teaspoon oregano
1 teaspoon cumin
½ teaspoon kosher salt

Toss the sesame seeds into a pan on medium-high heat to toast until golden brown, about 5 minutes. Remove to the side to cool down. Put the thyme, sumac, oregano, cumin, and salt in a bowl. Stir together. Once sesame seeds are cooled, add to the bowl, and mix. This blend lasts in a container for 1 month, and in the freezer for up to 6 months. Just make sure in both instances to remove as much air as possible.

·········· peak-season ··········
blender tomato sauce

Blender tomato sauce is exactly what it sounds like: put tomatoes in a blender with some garlic and olive oil and you've got a sauce! It avoids all the pitfalls and work of canning tomatoes while retaining the summer perfection. The key here is to only use the freshest, never-chilled, summer tomatoes. That summer flavor will shine through and make it all worth it. It's essentially like a chunky gazpacho in a sauce— bright, fresh, and full of life even when it's had a stint in the freezer.

Serving: 4–6

Ingredients
2 pounds ripe tomatoes
4 large garlic cloves
3 tablespoons extra-virgin olive oil
1 teaspoon salt
¼ teaspoon freshly ground black pepper

Add the tomatoes, garlic, olive oil, salt, and pepper into a blender and blend enough so that it has come together but is still a bit chunky. Don't worry if it looks frothy and pink; that will subside. You can choose to keep it a more or less chunky; if you want a smooth sauce, that also works. You can also remove the seeds before blending if you want, but I don't find it necessary.

Portion the sauce into freezer-safe containers and place them in the freezer. When you are ready to use the sauce, you can either defrost it in the fridge or in the microwave. Add the sauce to whatever pasta or dish you want.

pantry peanut-butter curry

<30 MINUTES **NO DEFROSTING** **Microwave-FRIENDLY ~ ~ ~**

This sauce couldn't claim to be anywhere near a traditional Thai curry, but I am constantly inspired by Thai cuisine's incredible ability to harmoniously meld sweet, salty, and sour flavors. This sauce aims to give you a quick version of that concept by taking the depth of flavor in a curry paste and smoothing it out with coconut milk and peanut butter, while adding a zing via the apple cider vinegar. I love having this sauce on hand because it turns almost anything into a star dish. Always keep some in your freezer for when you need to have a burst of flavor for your rice, noodles, and proteins.

Serving: 4–8

Ingredients
1 can coconut milk
2 tablespoons red curry paste
¼ cup peanut butter
½ tablespoon salt
2 tablespoons apple cider vinegar

Whisk all ingredients together. If you are eating now you can add it to whatever dish you are making.

If you are freezing it, freeze in separate portions (I like to freeze this sauce in silicone ice cube trays). When you are ready to use this curry, you can either let it defrost overnight in the fridge or heat it up in the microwave. Stir a bit to get the consistency back and serve immediately on top of whatever recipe you are using it in.

pie crust

Nothing is better to constantly have stashed in your freezer than a pie crust. Often, I'll do two, but you can even double this recipe to make four and just keep the discs ready to go in the freezer. They are so easy to make and freeze so well that there's never a reason to use store-bought again!

Serving: 2 pie crusts

Ingredients
2½ cups all-purpose flour
1 teaspoon salt
1½–2 tablespoons granulated sugar
1 cup (16 tablespoons) very cold unsalted butter
4–10 tablespoons ice-cold water

Combine the flour, salt, and sugar in a bowl. Grate the butter on a box grater into the flour mixture. Gently stir it together. You can use your hands but just be careful to keep the mixture as cool as possible so that the butter doesn't melt. You can also combine the dry ingredients with the butter in a food processor if that is easier for you. The butter should still be in pea-sized chunks when incorporated. Slowly add the water in and mix until it just comes together as a dough. The amount varies because it highly depends on the flour and butter you use. When it is ready, divide the dough in half and roll each half into a disc on a floured work surface using a rolling pin (an empty wine bottle also does the trick). Wrap each disc in plastic wrap and place in the freezer.

Before you are ready to use, place the pie crust(s) in the fridge for a few hours to thaw. Then, use the crust(s) as needed.

conversion charts

Metric and Imperial Conversions

(These conversions are rounded for convenience)

Ingredient	Cups/Tablespoons/ Teaspoons	Ounces	Grams/Milliliters
Butter	1 cup/ 16 tablespoons/ 2 sticks	8 ounces	230 grams
Cheese, shredded	1 cup	4 ounces	110 grams
Cream cheese	1 tablespoon	0.5 ounce	14.5 grams
Cornstarch	1 tablespoon	0.3 ounce	8 grams
Flour, all-purpose	1 cup/1 tablespoon	4.5 ounces/0.3 ounce	125 grams/8 grams
Flour, whole wheat	1 cup	4 ounces	120 grams
Fruit, dried	1 cup	4 ounces	120 grams
Fruits or veggies, chopped	1 cup	5 to 7 ounces	145 to 200 grams
Fruits or veggies, pureed	1 cup	8.5 ounces	245 grams
Honey, maple syrup, or corn syrup	1 tablespoon	0.75 ounce	20 grams
Liquids: cream, milk, water, or juice	1 cup	8 fluid ounces	240 milliliters
Oats	1 cup	5.5 ounces	150 grams
Salt	1 teaspoon	0.2 ounce	6 grams
Spices: cinnamon, cloves, ginger, or nutmeg (ground)	1 teaspoon	0.2 ounce	5 milliliters
Sugar, brown, firmly packed	1 cup	7 ounces	200 grams
Sugar, white	1 cup/1 tablespoon	7 ounces/0.5 ounce	200 grams/12.5 grams
Vanilla extract	1 teaspoon	0.2 ounce	4 grams

Oven Temperatures

Fahrenheit	Celsius	Gas Mark
225°	110°	¼
250°	120°	½
275°	140°	1
300°	150°	2
325°	160°	3
350°	180°	4
375°	190°	5
400°	200°	6
425°	220°	7
450°	230°	8

troubleshooting faqs

I get it. With the freezer, there often comes a bit of anxiety, so I wanted to create a section at the back to flip to when you just don't know where else to turn. Here are my frequently asked freezer questions:

Before Freezing

Can I refrigerate before I freeze?
Absolutely! You want to make sure you are freezing things only when they are room temperature or cold, because the faster food freezes the more intact it stays. Just make sure to know what is surrounding your food. If you put something super-hot into the fridge next to milk and eggs, you might heat those up, so just try not to put anything *too* hot in the fridge.

Do I really need a freezer-safe bag or container?
Not necessarily. Freezer-safe is usually just about how porous the material is. If air can't get in, it's freezer safe, so if you have a resealable bag that isn't labeled "freezer-safe," you may just want to double up materials to be extra careful.

Can I put glass in the freezer?
Only if it says freezer-safe (usually tempered glass). Otherwise, it can crack and that's no fun. Also make sure to remember that liquids expand, and glass has no wiggle room, so if you're freezing in a freezer-safe glass container, you still want to leave a little room at the top.

I really don't have time to cool my dish down. It won't be *that* bad if I just freeze it, right?
Please, please, *please* don't skip this crucial step. Nothing damages food more than going into a freezer hot. If you don't have time, just stick it in the fridge overnight or for a few hours, then freeze it when you do have time.

I want to stop wasting plastic bags and wrap—does anything else work just as well?
The only downside is cleanup, but otherwise there are tons of products that work just as well (if not better!) than single-use plastic. Many of the silicone bags and covers on the market are freezer-safe and very flexible and easy to use. Beeswax wraps are also good, but they are still a bit porous, so you may want to use another container around them if you are worried about air getting in. I am a huge fan of tempered glass containers as well because they can go straight from the freezer to the microwave or oven, which is usually easier than a disposable item anyway.

In-Freezer Issues

My food now has freezer burn. Is it still safe to eat?

Freezer burn doesn't make food go bad; it just makes it taste less appealing. You get freezer burn typically from food not being wrapped securely enough in an airtight container, so oxygen dehydrates the food. But you can still eat it and it certainly won't hurt you. If it's possible to cut the "burned" piece off, that usually helps a lot with flavor.

If I leave something super long in the freezer, is it bound to get freezer burn?

Not necessarily. If something is stored properly (no air getting in and staying at a consistent temperature), it only very gradually degrades. If you put in a few more minutes on the front-end of your storage plan, you can keep things for much longer than expected. If you are planning to do a longer storage, I would wrap in heavy-duty wrap, then put it in a container or bag for double the protection.

My food keeps getting freezer burn even though I stored it properly!

Check the temperature of your freezer. If it's not at or below 0°F, you might have a problem. Also make sure not to store anything too long in the doors of your freezer and try to not keep the freezer door open very long when you open it. Even a short time "outside" can start to defrost food, allowing it to then get freezer burn when the door closes again.

What do I do if I didn't write the date and I have no idea when I froze something?

Just use the best tools in your arsenal: your eyes and nose. If something was frozen properly it should be fine for a fairly long time, but there will be warning signs if something has gone off. Discoloration and freezer burn are usually the first clues, then if it smells off once it starts to defrost. But in general, as long as something has stayed frozen, it can't hurt you. (It just probably won't taste as good.)

Heating Back Up

I should have defrosted overnight but I didn't. What do I do?

There is no magic solution to forgetting to defrost. But to speed it up, put whatever food you are defrosting in a totally sealed container or bag (so absolutely no water can get in), then submerge it in a bowl of cold water. Don't try to be clever and defrost in hot water—you can semi-cook the outside and bacteria can start to grow if you aren't careful.

Do I have to defrost everything?

No! In fact, most of the recipes in this book don't need to defrost before cooking. Defrosting inevitably adds moisture back into your food and it can sit and get soggy. Oftentimes you are better off just cooking straight from frozen. So, unless the recipe specifically encourages it, I usually don't bother.

Why does the outside cook faster than the inside when reheating?

The most common reason for this is not storing your dishes in individual servings. If something is frozen as a giant block of ice, it takes much longer to heat up. If you did store your food in individual servings, try to stir it or break it apart in the middle of cooking. If you can't do that, or you are cooking meat, make sure your temperature isn't too high. You want to give it a more even heat.

Why is my pasta or food getting mushy when I reheat it?

There are two typical culprits. The first is overcooking it to start with. Pasta, lentils, crispier vegetables, and any other more delicate food needs to be frozen when it is just slightly undercooked (or al dente). Remember, every dish has residual heat, so if you remove your pasta when it tastes perfect in the pot, it's going to be soggier by the time it fully cools down. Remove your food from the heat before it is completely cooked, and you should save a lot of headache. The other mushy culprit is often not storing items in individual servings. The more food that there is to reheat, the longer it will take and the more the heat can overcook your food. So, make sure to start it off right before it goes in the freezer and you shouldn't have trouble!

Why does my food taste blander when it comes out of the freezer?

Freezing food can dull its flavor, so I often add a bit more salt if something doesn't taste quite as good when it comes out of the freezer, and that usually brings it back to life.

acknowledgments

First and foremost, thank you to my editor Nicole Mele and the whole Skyhorse team. You believed in this concept that I loved so dearly, and you let me run with it. Sharon Bowers, you are the honest cheerleader that every author needs (but rarely gets), and I am oh so grateful.

I am forever indebted to the dream team that worked on the photographs in this book: Noah Fecks, Ashton Keefe, Ethan Lunkenheimer, and Taylor Vance. I asked you to take a book of "brown frozen things" and somehow make it look beautiful without ever being unrealistic for people cooking at home. All your talent is only outweighed by your kindness.

Thank you to the incredible group of people who tested recipes in their kitchen and made this book profoundly better: Ainsley Moloney, Alison Corner, Amy Block, Anna Miller, Anna Hirsch-Holland, Barbara Paradise, Carrie Bachman, Carin Garland, Chris Miller, Danielle Yacovella, Diana Dosik Schwab, Diane Comforti, Elizabeth Conley, Emily Barber, Hilary Vandam, Juliet Izon, Jennifer Kelleher, Laura Duc, Laura Libby, Linnea Covington, Liz Slade, Lyn Boland, Molly Ahuja, Pamela Spiegel, Tamar Stearns, Tia Keenan, Tommy Grimes, Vanessa Nickerson, Veronique Trimble, Jude Walker, and Jenn Zicherman Kelleher. I am so grateful for your enthusiasm and time.

Friends don't come better than the people I have around me who are a part of this book through tasting, listening, and giving opinions. Thank you, Alana Rush, Alex Hammer Ducas, Alexis Adlouni, Carly Goldsmith, Emily O'Brien, Jane Bruce, Jess Chou, Marcy Franklin, Matt Kane, and Pia Desai. Thank you to Charlotte Druckman and Yasmin Fahr for sharing your cookbook wisdom, friendship, and for walks through COVID-19. Thank you to Stephenie Kammeyer for recipe inspiration and . . . well, you know the other thing.

Alison Taub, I'm so grateful to have you by my side. Ellie Bernal and Lucy Fernandes, thank you for having my back and loving our family so that I never worry about being a mom with a career. Thanks to Deiann Thomas and Avalon Salandy for being live-in taste testers during the craziest part of the pandemic (fish sticks forever). Yehuda, Natalie, Aaron, Leo, and Rachel—next year in each other's kitchens.

Annie, Will, Jon, and Skye—thank you for being the people I most love cooking for. Thursday night dinners are truly my happiest place. You guys have been giving commentary on these recipes and this crazy idea for *years*. And to my parents—it's all in the dedication.

The biggest thanks of all to my family. Daniel, Guy, Joy, and Rae, you make me complete—my ultimate taste testers and the loves of my life.

index